THE
LONGEST
SUICIDE

Other books by Jason Schneider

Have Not Been the Same: The CanRock Renaissance 1985-1995
(co-authored with Michael Barclay and Ian A.D. Jack)

3,000 Miles (A Novel)

Philip Snowcroft's Finality (A Novella)

*Whispering Pines: the Northern Roots of American Music
from Hank Snow to The Band*

Jason Schneider thanks:
Brian Kaufman, Brian Lynch, Heather Read, Phil Saunders, Phil Klygo,
Colin Smith, Gord Withers, Gord Celesta, Thor Henrickson, Scott Beadle,
Chris Wardman, Rob Hayter, Michael Barclay, Ian A.D. Jack, Kerry Doole,
David Farrell, Larry LeBlanc, James Keast, Ian Danzig, Michael Turner,
Alex Waterhouse-Hayward, Bev Davies, James O'Mara, Kate McBride,
Brad Paffe, Sharon Steele, Dee Lippingwell, Bob Hanham, Lou Molinaro,
the Simon Fraser University Vancouver Punk Collection, John Mackie,
Colin Brunton, Nardwuar the Human Serviette, Wendy Rofihe, and of course,
Art Bergmann for putting his trust in me to tell his story as best I could.

THE LONGEST SUICIDE

The Authorized Biography of Art Bergmann

by Jason Schneider

FOREWORD BY MICHAEL TURNER

anvil
PRESS

Anvil Press | Vancouver

For Sherri

Library and Archives Canada Cataloguing in Publication

Title: The longest suicide : the authorized biography of Art Bergmann / by Jason Schneider ;
    foreword by Michael Turner.
Names: Schneider, Jason, 1971- author. | Turner, Michael, 1962- writer of foreword.
Description: 1st edition
Identifiers: Canadiana 2022027083X | ISBN 9781772141962 (softcover)
Subjects: LCSH: Bergmann, Art. | LCSH: Rock musicians—Canada—Biography. | LCSH: Punk rock musicians—
    Canada—Biography. | LCSH: Singers—Canada—Biography.
Classification: LCC ML420 B498 S35 2022 | DDC 782.42166092—dc23

Book design by Derek von Essen

Represented in Canada by Publishers Group Canada
Distributed by Raincoast Books

The publisher gratefully acknowledges the financial assistance of the Canada Council for the Arts, the Canada Book Fund, and the Province of British Columbia through the B.C. Arts Council and the Book Publishing Tax Credit.

Anvil Press Publishers Inc.
P.O. Box 3008, Station Terminal
Vancouver, B.C. V6B 3X5
www.anvilpress.com

PRINTED AND BOUND IN CANADA

CONTENTS

Let's Go to Fuckin' Vancouver

The first time I heard the name Art Bergmann I was in the back seat of my mother's station wagon, en route to a family weekend at Cultus Lake, the radio suddenly blaring after my mother yanked out the 8-track mid-song (Stories' "Brother Louie") because the lyrics were upsetting my aunt. The dial was set to 1410 CFUN, I think—the tail end of a news story about a Vancouver band that had to change its name because the company it took it from was worried the band would tarnish its corporate image. The new name of the band, "according to its leader, Art Bergmann," is The Young Canadians; its dead name, the K-Tels.

The coincidence of this dead name band and the maker of the 8-track compilation—K-Tel's *Superstars Greatest Hits* (1974)—was not lost on my nervous aunt, who, in my recollection, took possession of all coincidences, as if they were her doing. "Can you believe it!" she kept saying. "It's like I'm magic or something!" And while I too was struck by the coincidence, it was years before I saw the circumstances concerning my introduction to this extraordinary artist—litigated from one band name to the next—as typical of a career that was in inverse proportion to his talent. For there is, to my mind, no greater story in the history of Canadian music than the tragic career of Arthur Frank Bergmann.

I entered Grade 12 in the fall of that year, 1979. I was aware of punk—its music, its attitude, its accoutrements—and had seen and heard its influence at my high school and had noted its tentative presence on the streets of Vancouver. I say tentative because it took a lot of nerve to be punked-out in Vancouver in the late 1970s, when the punks of the day occasionally came in contact with the port city's throwback greasers, who took it upon themselves to challenge any stranger who, like them, wore stovepipe jeans, black motorcycle jackets, and short hair. For those looking to read a picture-perfect account of this crossover, I refer you to John Armstrong's *Guilty of Everything* (2003), the chapter where he and Art attend a Mitch Ryder concert in Gastown—a concert that, on the topic of inversions, was the inverse of the Yardbirds concert scene in Antonioni's *Blow-Up* (1966).

As with any scene there are resident experts, and the expert on punk at our school was Dave Trotter, who first played for me the K-Tels' "Hawaii." Penned by Art and co-author Ross Carpenter, "Hawaii" was a catchy yet confusing tune because it broke from the Sex Pistols' directive to forsake a "holiday in the sun" and visit instead the Berlin Wall ("the new Belsen"), to "see some history," while the K-Tels, in contrast, where asking us to join them ("Let's go to fuckin' Hawaii"). Not wanting to break from the program, I kept the contradiction to myself, only to realize years later that what Art and Ross were *saying* was in fact truer to the anarchic politic of punk, a dialectical extension of the burlesque, with its rock-on-water assault on the mainstream. Johnny Rotten was aware of this too, when he derided the Pistol's manager, Malcolm McLaren, for comparing the Pistols to the Situationists of the 1960s.

Art was a local celebrity by the time I first saw him in person. Not at a club or in a concert setting, not yet, but crossing Robson Street in front of the Art Gallery. This was sometime in the mid-to-late 1980s, after I had read enough about Art to know he was working with local music mogul Sam Feldman and had signed a major label record deal. This sighting is a retinal burn for me because Art was someone who had by then built up enough myth to be beholden to it, and we all know what it is to see someone we "know of" for the first time in person. But again, the contradiction: a bed-headed Art on a woman's fixed-gear bicycle, at least two sizes too small, dressed in a white undershirt, black jeans, and flip-flops—in one hand, the bicycle's handlebar; in the other, a black Samsonite briefcase. An older man, clearly a tourist, attempted to take his picture, a gesture that woke Art from his stupor and, after three powerful pumps of the chain wheel, he disappeared around the corner, heading north on Hornby.

My first conversation with Art came in January 1993. I was by then a seasoned musician, having co-founded Hard Rock Miners six years earlier, but was now spending more time writing books and giving readings than I was on recording and touring. Eager to find a new way of presenting writing and music together, I approached Janet Forsyth at the Railway Club, and she offered me the last Monday of the month for what I was calling the Reading Railroad. I had already lined up poets Evelyn Lau, Judy Radul, and Peter Trower, but for my musical guest I wanted a songwriter with some literariness, and I could think of no one better than Art. Janet kindly gave me Art's number, and I phoned him first thing in the afternoon. I have no recollection of our conversation, but I remember it was closer to Gertrude Stein than any contract negotiation. I had never seen Art Bergmann solo acoustic before, and was surprised he agreed to appear that way. The event was an astounding success, and because I promised everyone an equal share of the door, Art was equally astounded when I handed him $400 cash.

Though enamoured with Art, I can't say this was the beginning of a long-lasting friendship. From our brief dealings, I sensed Art was someone who was uneasy with the world, or at least easily exasperated by it. This became evident the next time I called on him, a couple months before the publication of my second book, *Hard Core Logo* (1993). My publisher had asked if I could find someone to write a jacket blurb, and of course I thought of Art. In fact, I thought a lot about Art during the writing of *Hard Core Logo*; not as someone to blurb the book, but as the basis for one of its characters, Bucky Haight, the legendary "proto-punk" who withdraws from the "hellfire of the music business" to lead a slower, meditative life in a Prairie farmhouse. Sure enough, when Sherri opened the door and invited me into her and Art's Oak Street apartment, I could see that interior life writ large in their extensive collection of books, with Art curled up reading Timothy Findley's *The Wars* (1977). Art said he would read the manuscript and have something for me when I returned the following week.

It wasn't until my second visit to Art and Sherri's that Art's life came into focus. Like that earlier phone call, I have little recollection of what was said, but like my sighting of Art on Robson that day, I have a crystal-clear image of him in a light blue V-neck sweater sitting at the kitchen table rubbing his forehead, appalled no doubt that I had asked him to read my manuscript and produce from it a single line of hype. Sherri, a journalist, was helpful here, for she explained to Art what a blurb is, how it is supposed to function and why, in this instance, he should cough one up. And as this was going on, I sat in silence, travelling the landscape of Art's remarkable face, a face that alternated from deadpan mannequin to twisted incredulity, a tortured face that belonged less to Art than to the slag heap of History, occasionally breaking from itself to stare sideways, beyond the frame, like Klee's *Angelus Novus* (1920). A transformative experience for me, after which, to quote another Vancouver musical act (Slow), "I have not been the same."

I left Hard Rock Miners in June 1993, and in August of that year I opened the Malcolm Lowry Room at the North Burnaby Inn, a hotel so notorious that it, like the K-Tels, was forced to change its name. Originally named the Admiral (a name it has since returned to), the NBI was a two-storey biker haunt with a 250-seat strip bar to the east of its lobby, and to the west of it, a 99-seat lounge that was mine to do with as I dared. Above it all, a U-shaped floor of hotel rooms filled with pensioners, parolees, and assorted peripatetics. Of course it wasn't long before I booked Art to play the first of three solo shows there, all of them drawing diehard Art fans, but also those curious to see how much weirder his audience could get. As per our "contract," I gave Art and Sherri a room for the night upstairs, and other mysterious residents were coaxed down to hear Art play, along with a menagerie of bikers, punks, suits, jocks, hippies, and little black dresses.

The last time I saw Art was at the Commodore Ballroom, for the filming of the Bucky Haight benefit concert that comes near the beginning of Bruce McDonald's *Hard Core Logo* (1996). Joining Art on the bill were contemporaries D.O.A. and the Modernettes, as well as younger acts Flash Bastard and Lick the Pole. Much of the filming took place backstage, where Art is hugged by Hard Core Logo band members as the starry-eyed younger bands look on. I have no recollection if Art and I spoke to each other, apart from a shared eye-roll or two, though I remember being surprised by how comfortable he was with these semi-improvised scenes. Whether this had anything to do with Art performing *for real* that night, I don't know. Maybe this time the incredulity was mine, beholden as I was to my own meta mythmaking.

I've thought a lot about Art Bergmann these past twenty-five years. Sometimes these thoughts come to me on my own, like when I am stuck on a song lyric and I ask myself, "What would Art do?" Other times when running into people from my club days, where Art's name invariably comes up. Everyone who at least knows of Art has a story to tell: how his albums were never as "good" as the demos that preceded them, how his managers or A&R reps never understood him well enough to allow him to succeed on *their terms*, how everyone expected him to embody a lifestyle that was so boring to him that he had no choice but to give them the worst version possible. Indeed, I can't think of anyone from Vancouver's punk era whose life and career is as pathologized as Art Bergmann's. Naturally some of this is of Art's doing, for it was Art, after all, who asked us to join him on his musical journeys to Hawaii, Tahiti, Miami, Las Vegas…

Speaking of Las Vegas, Art's "Bound for Vegas" (1990) came on the radio while I was waiting for my mom at the booster clinic last November. Great song, I thought, as I always think when I hear it. But those lines—"I'm a never-was trying to be a has-been / A has-been out on the comeback trail"—those lines are as great as anything ever written. And when I heard them this last time, I thought about what it is to commit yourself to a life in music or writing or film or dance or visual art; that no matter how that life goes, what you get as you enter the last third of it is the story of that journey; and how that story is, in our post-commodity relational auto-fictive moment, our one true art. The story of Art Bergmann's career is perceived by many to be a succession of failures, but the story of Art's life? If Art doesn't have the best story, it is always the most magical.

Michael Turner, February 2022

(Kenneth Locke)

OLD TRUTHS NEVER DIE

If it hadn't been for the Russian Revolution, I wouldn't be here.

FRANZ "FRANK" BERGMANN NEVER FORGOT the sound of bullets hitting the train. They struck in rapid succession as his family escaped the bands of Bolsheviks and anarchists (it hardly mattered who was doing the killing) that were intent on asserting authority across southern Russia. The area encompassed sites that had been granted to Mennonite communities by Empress Catherine II in the late eighteenth century, but with Bolshevik party leader Vladimir Lenin seizing power over a hundred years later, the endgame of Russia's peasant class overcoming a thousand years of indentured servitude to generations of tsars fully got under way. Frank's family belonged to the Ukrainian Mennonite faction, and like many other families had migrated from Germany and prospered through religious freedom and pacifism. Now they were easy targets of revenge for those emboldened in the wake of Lenin's Red Army claiming a decisive victory in the Russian Civil War, leading to the creation of the Soviet Union in 1922.

Frank was born August 14, 1913, in the village of Dmitrovka, near Arkadak, halfway between the Caucasus region and Moscow. As an outpost in the grain trade, the area was a priority for the Bolsheviks to secure in the early 1920s, although atrocities against Mennonites, as well as the affluent private landowners known as *kulaks*, began as early as 1919 in Ukraine, perpetrated in large degree by anarchist Nestor Makhno's peasant army that robbed and killed with little resistance. Frank witnessed that carnage up close one day when he stumbled upon a ten-year-old neighbour lying dead in a field. For Mennonites, the only response to the societal chaos was emigration, and that choice came for the Bergmann family during the summer of 1923.

Russian Mennonites had begun making long, arduous journeys to Canada and Latin America in the 1870s, mainly in reaction to laws enacted for mandatory military service. Those numbers dramatically increased in the aftermath of the revolution, aided by established Canadian Mennonite groups, which obtained permission from the federal government to expedite the immigration process on the condition that new arrivals develop parcels of farmland for specific lengths of time. A further deal was struck with the Canadian Pacific Railway company to provide safe passage, which included one of its ocean liners, RMS *Empress of France*. On July

17, 1923, after making their way through Europe to Southampton, England, Frank and his family boarded the CPR ship, and landed at Quebec City within a week.

From there, the seemingly endless journey westward continued to Manitoba, where they connected with "Old Colony" members of the faith who dubbed the latest waves of arrivals "Russlanders" for their relatively advanced levels of education and progressive attitudes. After a brief period of acclimatizing to their new land, the Russlanders then had to decide on their next destination, where land was available to purchase or lease under agreeable conditions. Handfuls of families would most often band together, pushing on westward to Saskatchewan and Alberta, where the vast, flat expanses were in many ways a reminder of home.

It was not only Russian Mennonites who were immigrating to Canada in large numbers during this period. The exodus from Germany had been constant as well since the late nineteenth century, with new communities establishing themselves across the Prairies. It was in Tiefengrund, Saskatchewan—located on an isolated stretch between Saskatoon and Prince Albert—that Elder Peter Regier settled around 1894. He had been ordained a bishop in West Prussia seven years earlier, and he envisioned establishing a new congregation of his Rosenort Mennonite Church in the area, eventually attracting more Regiers and their extended families and friends to emigrate. Many churches were built during the ensuing two decades, and many babies were born. Among them was Edith Selma Regier, who arrived on December 9, 1917.

In the late 1920s, advertisements started appearing in local newspapers throughout the Prairie provinces offering available land in the Fraser Valley just outside Vancouver, British Columbia, where the primary attraction was a more hospitable climate. It was enough to persuade some residents of Tiefengrund, including Edith Regier's sister, who, once their schooling was completed, brought her along on a journey westward over the Rockies to where new congregations had been established in Abbotsford, Surrey, Aldergrove, and elsewhere throughout the 1930s. It was the area where Frank Bergmann's family had already settled and, now an adult and free to follow his own path, the bleak realities of the Great Depression had little to do with strictly adhering to any religious beliefs. Mere survival was paramount, and achieving that forced Frank to strike out on his own with whatever skills he possessed.

Frank was a competent carpenter, and got better at it with each job he found, eventually landing in Vancouver where there was steady work for those capable of doing it. Meanwhile, as Edith reached adulthood, she was drawn to the city as well by job opportunities. As Germany, the country their ancestors had once fled, launched its war against the rest of Europe, Edith found solace in a young man she'd met whose world view had been formed by empathy for those who remained trapped within the madness unfolding there. Frank and Edith were married in Vancouver on February 10, 1940, and, using all of their savings, found a parcel of land southeast of the city in Cloverdale, where Frank built a house for the family next to Lord Tweedsmuir High School—later Lord Tweedsmuir Secondary—that would ultimately secure his status in his adopted country.

Three sons, Anton (known as Tony), Joseph Conrad, and Carl were born within a three-year span after the Bergmanns' marriage, before they welcomed a fourth, Arthur Frank Bergmann, on February 8, 1953. Later, he would like to say that among his first memories was

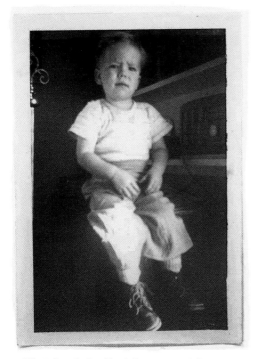

The infant Arthur Frank Bergmann, 1953.

At age five, with younger brother Hans.

hearing Elvis Presley sing "How Great Thou Art," but the rendition he most likely heard was by his church's congregation. Within a few years, Art and the fifth brother who followed him, Hans, were part of that choir, dressed in their best clothes, including bow ties.

I had a totally happy childhood. My dad was working his ass off as a carpenter and he added on to the house each time another kid was born. Everyone had to take piano lessons and there were recitals. And we all had to sing in church—German hymns—which is how I guess I learned about harmony. There was music around the house all the time. Dad played the mandolin, and Mom played the piano and had a really powerful, operatic voice, which could be annoying. You don't really know music until you learn how to appreciate it and deconstruct it, which I did later on. But it was always there, gospel music booming through the house. Saturday afternoons, it was live from the Metropolitan Opera House. Dad thought music died after Beethoven.

Despite the children gaining an appreciation of music at home, there was nothing Frank could do to stem the tide of alien sounds rushing over the border in the mid-1950s, sounds that would implore his beloved Ludwig Van to roll over and tell Tchaikovsky the news. His eldest sons fell victim as soon as they caught snippets of it on the radio waves emanating from Vancouver, where in 1954 sixteen-year-old Robert "Red" Robinson became the first DJ to spread this strange new music in Canada, via station CJOR. Robinson's influence increased exponentially three years later, after he moved to the powerhouse top-40 station CKWX, which partnered with Vancouver promoters in bringing the new stars of rock and roll to venues like Empire Stadium and the Georgia Auditorium. Robinson was there to introduce them, making him a star in his own right and making the records he played highly sought-after.

The eldest Bergmann brothers hunted them all diligently each time they got the chance to venture into downtown Vancouver and dig through the racks of 45-rpm singles at places like Woodward's department store on West Hastings Street. They'd return home to Cloverdale with the latest hits by Elvis, Buddy Holly, Eddie Cochran, and anyone else whose name appeared under the soon-to-be familiar logos of Sun Records and other American labels that had found a way to infiltrate Canada. And with the music came the rebellious lifestyle, much to Frank Bergmann's frustration.

> It must have been really tough on him, coming from his background and having my older brothers get into rock and roll and drinking in the late '50s. They were my heroes because of the records they would bring home and play in the basement. My dad couldn't get his head wrapped around any of it and that's when a lot of problems started happening. He was always a believer in "Spare the rod, spoil the child" and all of that, but once my brothers were in high school it got a lot worse. There was one time when we went to Saskatchewan for a summer vacation, but my second-oldest brother, who was sixteen, didn't come along. When we got back, the house was totally destroyed—windows were smashed and a lot of my things were wrecked. That was a real eye-opening moment for me, trying to comprehend what would possess my brother to do something like that.

By the time Art entered Cloverdale Junior High, his oldest brother, Tony, had moved on from his rock and roll rebellion, marrying a woman from a Jehovah's Witnesses family and converting to their beliefs. The next in line, Joe, likewise landed on the straight and narrow path, finding a career as an accountant for Revenue Canada. The third brother, Carl, eventually adopted the controversial Kabalarian Philosophy and changed his name to Neall Calvert in accordance with the group's belief in the connection between names and numerology.

Art's own rebellious phase kicked into gear in the mid-1960s as he began high school at Abbotsford Senior Secondary, spurred by the new interpreters of the music that had turned his brothers away from the tenets of their upbringing. These were the records on which Art now spent his weekly allowance at a Cloverdale variety store where nothing was priced over a dollar—singles by the Beatles, Stones, and Kinks, anything that fanned the flames of his growing sense of independence. As Art became engrossed in creating his new identity, Frank, perhaps feeling the weight of Art's brothers being led astray, assumed the job of running a Mennonite home for foster children in Abbotsford, some of whom he took in personally.

Those were some damaged kids, girls and boys. That was during two years while I was in high school, which is an immense period of time when you're fifteen and sixteen. Suddenly, I was involved with these JDs—juvenile delinquents. The first time I did acid was with one of those kids. It was like driving with Ferris wheels spinning in front of my eyes. My parents had made an arrangement with their church, and there were social workers around all the time. But kids would be coming and going at all hours of the night. That was when South Surrey started to become a very, very wild place. Cloverdale, with a population of maybe two thousand, became the drug capital of Surrey. They'd be cutting up drugs in the old pool hall, right on the counter. And there was everything from marijuana to heroin. It was unbelievable.

There was this other wild crew that lived out in the valley, at this place called Mount Lehman. There was a family there, the Skantzes, that owned about sixty acres with cabins kind of scattered around. Kids ended up moving in there and they basically could do anything their hearts desired. One of the Skantz boys, Anders—who we called Andy and who was also the president of the student council—proclaimed himself the mayor. My friends and I usually ended up there every weekend and things would tend to get primitive. We'd all be drinking from gallon jugs of Calona Royal Red wine—some that would be loaded up with 900 mics of pure LSD.

Art was careful not to completely give himself over to hedonism, though, taking jobs whenever opportunities arose to balance his school work. He was game for anything, from construction to painting, and although earning a paycheque was always nice, it was secondary to the hold that rock and roll now had on him. Unlike his older brothers, Art recognized the crack in the door the British bands had opened by showing that this was music anyone could play if they had enough courage to give it a shot.

His father ultimately came to realize that too, as the world he once knew forever changed in the late 1960s. The punishments suddenly decreased, and on the occasions when Art came to him to borrow money, his response stemmed directly from the Bible, specifically Luke 11:11: "What father among you, if your son asks for bread, would give him a stone?"

As long as his children worked as hard at pursuing their goals as he had with his carpentry, Frank was happy. And when his days of making a living through manual labour began to wane, he channelled his energy into a new passion for writing about his Mennonite community and the social justice issues in which he firmly believed. In 1973, Frank shared the wisdom he'd accrued throughout his life in a lengthy article published in *Maclean's* magazine entitled "A Workingman Serves His Own Master," a powerfully eloquent tribute to anyone who laboured with their hands.

"Things have no status in themselves, nor can they confer it on their owners, but they carry a patina of humanness that should be respected," Frank wrote. "They were created, not by directors meeting in a boardroom, not by market analysts, not by salesmen, but by the touch of human hands for the use and convenience and enjoyment of other human beings.

"It is the evolution of the middleman between maker and user that has put FOR SALE signs on all things lovely, and led to the rejection of the market society by so many of our children. But old truths never die and ancient certitudes are never quite forgotten. There are new listeners to the words of Krishna, written in the Bhagavad Gita 2,500 years ago: 'Let the wise man work unselfishly for the good of all the world.'"

Frank concluded with words that seemed to foreshadow his son's attitude toward what would soon become his vocation. "Meantime the workman, whose employer views him as nothing more than some unruly, self-willed machine, to be turned on and off at the whim of market pressures, can keep his sanity only by looking at the products of his hands as a contribution to humankind and not as an item for sale. Only by desiring to do things well can he remain a creator and not become a slave."

With parents Frank and Edith Bergmann. (ALEX WATERHOUSE-HAYWARD)

FRIDAY ON MY MIND

To a non-resident, Surrey BC may simply be Vancouver's largest suburb, but its town centres such as Cloverdale, along with the bordering cities of White Rock and Langley—conceived on the nineteenth-century British model of urban planning—have each bred their own distinct culture. At least, that's how it was in the 1960s, when territory began being marked by different groups and conflicts among them consistently flared.

In White Rock, where kids could traditionally throw all-night parties with bonfires on the beach, the spectre of the Gypsy Wheelers motorcycle gang hung over the town once it had established a clubhouse and set about dominating the local drug trade. In Langley, it was common to see holdovers from rock and roll's big bang ruling the streets—blue-collar thugs who still sculpted their hair with grease and seemed adamant to live in a *Wild One*-style world where any perceived slight was enough cause for a rumble. More often than not, those on the receiving end were unfortunate suburban hippies who soon got the message that a peace-and-love philosophy was not a practical defence.

Those lessons were frequently learned at musical events, something Art faced head-on at age sixteen in the summer of 1969, when, like many others, he felt the irresistible pull of the Vancouver Pop Festival, held at the Paradise Valley Resort in Squamish. With their August 22–24 schedule, the weekend immediately following the Woodstock festival, organizers faced the same challenges as their New York counterparts in terms of cost overruns and resistance from local authorities. However, it was estimated that only a fraction of Woodstock's turnout was there to see a ragtag lineup highlighted by Little Richard, blues rockers (and Woodstock vets) Canned Heat, rising homegrown stars the Guess Who, and a new group of Frank Zappa protégés fronted by a singer calling himself Alice Cooper. Only a few weeks later, at the Toronto Rock 'n' Roll Revival, Cooper would make national headlines by throwing a live chicken into the audience, whereupon it was promptly torn to pieces.

I hitchhiked there just to be able to see all of these artists at the same time. It seemed like every band in the world was playing. I remember hearing "Sympathy for the Devil" on the radio, which was a profound moment.

When we got there, we snuck under the security fence, and that night it got so cold up in the mountains that the security guards were burning anything they could to keep warm. All of us had acute cannabis intoxication. Nobody was getting paid, but the bands played all night. That was the first time seeing Gram Parsons and the Flying Burrito Brothers. They played at 3 in the morning and sounded just like the record. I remember they actually calmed things down, because it was a pretty tense scene up until then. But for a kid, man, a festival like that was gold.

For others, though, the presence of motorcycle gang members, some of whom aggressively opposed the use of hallucinogens and those taking them, was responsible for perpetuating a state of fear the entire weekend. A report in the *Squamish Times* in the aftermath stated: "Many of the young people who attended the festival were dismayed and shocked at some of the activities that accompanied it; or which were noticed there. Some have said they have no desire to attend another one. This is good, and perhaps the best way for the young people to discover a sense of values."

If the festival instilled any values within Art, they were instead a reflection of rock and roll's power to unleash previously suppressed wells of emotion, particularly when it came to Little Richard, then mounting a comeback of sorts alongside many of his 1950s peers. He'd adapted to the times by adorning himself in more outlandish contemporary costumes, yet he continued to pound the piano and wail "Tutti Frutti" with unbridled fury as a torrent of sweat cascaded from his impossibly coiffed pompadour. It had been only a decade since his last flurry of hit singles, but such was the rapid progression of music during the 1960s that many kids Art's age already considered Richard an amusing curiosity from a different age. Still, Art had never lost the connection that had been established when he heard his older brothers play Little Richard records. Now, having seen Richard in person, still more than capable of whipping a crowd into a frenzy—and mocking the bikers who hurled racist taunts at him—Art instinctively knew that whatever his own music was going to be, it needed to contain whatever Little Richard's essence was.

The budding young rocker, circa 1968.

Although Art's piano lessons lasted until Grade 5, and his next instrument had been the trumpet, he had moved to the guitar when he was thirteen. With his grounding in basic music theory, Art applied himself to learning how to play it through a Mel Bay instructional book and in short order could strum the chords to the Kingston Trio's "Tom Dooley." From there, he learned rhythm from Buddy Holly and Bo Diddley records, providing him with just enough necessary technique to join up with some fellow teens in 1967 in a band they dubbed Blind Truth.

To call it a band is generous, though, as it was more an excuse for Art and some school friends that included drummer Randy Mathers (late of the local pipe and drum corps) and fellow budding guitarist Art Panchishin to get together and make some noise. As Panchishin remembered, "Art didn't know how to play guitar when I met him, but I showed him a few chords and he took off like a rocket. He was really a brainiac; in school, he didn't even have to study to get As."

Although rudimentary, their attempts to play rock and roll sufficiently impressed a lot of other kids, and Mathers recalled them jamming primarily at a rundown building close to the US border crossing that served as a primary teen hangout spot commonly known as "the orphanage." "I believe Blind Truth may have only played for the other kids at the orphanage, I don't believe we ever actually had a gig," Mathers said. "But Art was completely into playing music, even at that time, and looking back now I'm not surprised at all that he followed his own path."

Despite Art's enthusiasm for all the British Invasion bands, he still had a lot to learn about getting the sound right. At least, that was according to one of the musicians in his circle of friends, Bill Laurie, who knew how to harmonize, played a Hofner bass made famous by Paul McCartney, and sought to put together a proper British Invasion–style band. It led Laurie, Panchishin, and Mathers to form the Young Society, which attained a brief period of notoriety in the Lower Mainland during 1968 and '69 through a single, "Games" b/w "Flyin' Away," recorded at Mushroom Studios in Vancouver and pressed on studio owner Al Reusch's Arrex label.

Yet, as was the case with most 1960s garage bands, notoriety was fleeting for the Young Society, as innovative new sounds fully transformed the musical ecosystem. It was a case of adapt or die, and for Art that meant taking the next step with his guitar playing. He started getting together regularly with Panchishin, who taught him how to play the common blues scale on the 1962 Fender Stratocaster Art had purchased from his brother Joe, the guitar being a holdover from a time when the eldest Bergmann brothers half-heartedly attempted to form a band. Panchishin said, "By then, I was playing my Gibson, and Art had his Stratocaster, so that was an indication to me of how serious he was about playing. I basically showed him how to do a few more intricate things so he wasn't just playing chords at a hundred miles an hour all the time."

Armed with this new-found knowledge, Art set to practising for up to six hours a day and getting together with Andy Skantz in Mount Lehman, where the idea of forming a new band emerged out of their frequent LSD trips. Skantz was still a wild child, a trait that naturally seemed to attract Art's friendship, and he often had no misgivings about performing in the nude or coming up with songs such as "Greaseball Baby (But I Sure Do Fuckin' Get Around)." Skantz suggested they call themselves the Mt Lehman Grease Band.

Panchishin recalled of that first, short-lived 1969 incarnation: "That band was very much made up of a bunch of drinkers and party animals. I would smoke a little bit but I was never much of a drinker, so I couldn't believe how they could find these places to play after some of the crap that happened. I was pretty laid back and I didn't want to hurt myself. I was more concerned about my hands than anything else."

> I learned how to play the blues, and it's a great way for a white kid to start off, but you can't do what those [blues artists] did. I mean, they never played the same measures or beats from one verse to the next, especially Robert Johnson. With people like Eric Clapton, it became a cut-and-dried twelve-bar form and they really dumbed it down. The blues is really something ephemeral, and the best of those artists are beyond genius. But back then, I thought the guy who taught me to play that stuff was a wizard. At the same time, I most enjoyed whatever was on the radio, really. I was a big fan of the Byrds, Motown, and even stuff like "You Don't Own Me" by Lesley Gore. Every night, I'd listen to CFUN, 1410 AM in Vancouver and their DJs John Tanner and J.B. Shayne. Pop music was great back then, but it became really interesting when you could hear psychedelic influences starting to creep in. I was a mini-hippie for a while. I really liked Jefferson Airplane, and I had a thing for Grace Slick. But then there were songs like "Friday on My Mind" by the Easybeats, which is brilliantly constructed, and to me is still the ultimate teen anthem.

Skantz was simply too feral to be in a band, so Art soon turned to other friends at Abbotsford Senior Secondary, such as David Mitchell, known by the nickname Mitzo, to try to get something more substantial off the ground as the new decade began. Mitchell's father had moved his family to Abbotsford from Vancouver to stem the influence of some of his shadier business affiliations, but the unstoppable force of rock and roll still got control of his son. "We lived at a time when everyone we knew either wanted to be, or was, in a rock and roll band," Mitchell said. "But the gang that Art and I convened, we were interested in kind of reviving rock and roll in its purest form. We weren't really interested in the direction music was going in at that time. What we were interested in was traditional rock and roll, and I guess we could have been considered a precursor to the punk rock movement, even though it would still obviously be a while before people started using that term."

For Mitchell, a big part of the impetus behind forming a band with Art was that, even at seventeen, he recognized his friend's prodigious talent, particularly in an ability to play Chuck Berry licks, something Art mastered through a painstaking process of dissecting his record collection note for note. Such dedication was beyond the scope of most of their fellow students; instead, the pair began attracting outside characters with common interests until a new Mt

Lehman Band took shape, with Mitchell falling into the role of lead singer, Tony Pratt joining on bass, and fourteen-year-old Murphy Farrell manning the drum kit.

"I was in awe of Art," said Heather Haley, a couple of years behind him at school. "Cloverdale was a small town, and even smaller back then, but Art was playing music for as long as I'd been aware of him. I was an aspiring singer and musician, but he was really doing it."

At first, Art's parents allowed his band to practise at their house, and Mitchell recalled a warm family atmosphere, with the musicians often included in large dinners alongside both Art's biological siblings and the foster children. But upon finishing their Grade 12 year, Art, Mitchell, and the rest of the band rented a house near White Rock, which for a year became ground zero for their creative emergence, as well as party central.

> At our graduation [in the spring of 1971], Mitzo gave the principal a handshake with the middle finger. None of us went to the dance. We went to the jungle—Mount Lehman. I guess it was a boycott of the parades and dresses of old. Who else did this? Apparently nobody.

The fully constituted Mt Lehman Grease Band—or sometimes simply the Mt Lehman Band—established a notorious reputation from the first time they staged shows at venues like the tiny Mount Lehman Community Hall, more accustomed to holding wedding receptions and town meetings. "Very quickly, almost spontaneously, we developed quite a cult following," Mitchell said. "Whenever we'd play, people from all kinds of groups would come, from hippies to greasers to bikers, and they would all go berserk because the music we were playing was pretty loud and wild."

For a time, the band was able to rent other community halls in the area for shows, or rely on friends who styled themselves as "managers" to book them for high-school dances or lunch-hour concerts, along with occasional slots opening for more well-known artists in the Lower Mainland. But as word spread of the damage that ensued from most of these gigs, people stopped returning their phone calls.

"That was the reason why we changed our name so often," Mitchell admitted. "The halls would just get trashed after we played. The high-school shows were always interesting because often people with no connection to the school would show up en masse and there would be drinking and dope smoking. It would drive the teachers and administrators crazy. I would usually take off my shirt because we'd always work up a sweat when we played, and at one school I remember the principal threatening to turn the power off unless I put my shirt back on. I was ready to pack up because of that, and told the audience that the show was going to be stopped because the principal was too turned on by my body. Of course, they all started booing, and it was actually Art who finally convinced me to put my shirt back on because he wanted to keep playing."

Although the Mt Lehman Band did its fair share of vintage rock and roll covers and new standards by the Rolling Stones and others, they were also adamant about playing as much original material as they could get away with. The bulk of the songs came from Art, with

Mitchell sometimes contributing lyrics and the entire band collaborating on the end results during rehearsals at the White Rock house.

> Our hit was "Pissin' the Blues," with the chorus "Pissin', shittin', jackin', blowin', rubbin' my load on the bathroom wall." To hear a room full of kids screaming this was nirvana indeed. As far as content goes, we were very far from political. I wasn't very confident as a songwriter at the time, and you could say that my lyrics were somewhat misdirected.

Even then, Art had a clear vision of himself playing something akin to a Keith Richards role, crafting songs around thick, rhythmic chords rather than attempting any "guitar god" antics, despite being quite capable of that as well. It seemed any guitarist hoping to attract attention at that point needed to possess such a bag of tricks because of the precedent set by Jimi Hendrix, who coincidentally spent parts of his childhood in Vancouver, living with his grandmother when life with his parents in Seattle proved too chaotic. Vancouver's proximity to San Francisco also made it an early destination for that city's psychedelic bands, creating a cultural exchange that by 1967 led to a thriving hippie community centred around 4th Avenue's Psychedelic Shop and The Afterthought (a.k.a. the Kitsilano Theatre) where bands like the Grateful Dead and Jefferson Airplane first played in Vancouver. "I think 1968 might have been the craziest year," CFUN DJ John Tanner remembered. "That's when everybody and their dog came to the city to see the hippies and drive up 4th Avenue." Tanner began his CFUN stint in 1964 at age 21, and from then on had a ringside seat for the era's musical shifts as he emceed shows by everyone from the Beatles and Herman's Hermits to the Who and the Doors. "What was really incredible was that it happened so fast," Tanner added. "Vancouver had much more in common with the US west coast than with Toronto or Montreal at that time. California was a huge influence."

Tanner was ultimately fired from CFUN in 1968, not because of any music he played, but for an on-air exchange he'd had about British Columbia's then new licence plates that combined letters and numbers for the first time. One listener called in to say they'd spotted one that began with "FUK," and Tanner's fate was sealed. However, listeners could still enjoy an eclectic music mix from J.B. Shayne, who was basically given carte blanche by CFUN's young program director, Terry David Mulligan. But the rise of FM radio at the end of the decade became too much of a tempting option for Tanner, Shayne, and other on-air talent once Vancouver's CKLG became Canada's first FM rock station in March 1968. The hosts who defected there naturally brought their listenership with them, and the looser format allowed more of their personal tastes to be revealed.

Amid the endless fuzzed-out tracks famously popularized by early FM radio, like Iron Butterfly's "In-A-Gadda-Da-Vida," Shayne would occasionally drop in a song by one of his favourite bands, the Velvet Underground, whose dark, often grating sounds were widely considered the antithesis of the west coast aesthetic. When Art found Shayne's show on CKLG, he quickly realized what he was hearing was offering a window into a world he'd previously encountered in fleeting glimpses. It was difficult to even consider the Velvet Underground's "Heroin" rock and roll; it was more like a modern folk ballad in the sense of a narrator telling his story and giving the listener the opportunity to form their own opinion, for better or worse. The terrifying life described in Lou Reed's masterpiece was light years away from what most people in the Fraser Valley could relate to, but the song's inherent desperation —conveyed not only in its lyrics, but also in its two chords, which ebbed and flowed like someone's futile attempt to escape a straitjacket—spoke to a universal desire for freedom from oppression. Yes, this could be achieved through religion, Art had been taught, but heroin offered a more expedient path.

Then there was that strange country-and-western song that had stuck with Art since the Vancouver Pop Festival, a song that warned of the Lord's burning rain coming to cleanse the world of those who ignored the Bible's warning that you cannot serve both God and Mammon. The imagery in "Sin City" by the Flying Burrito Brothers made as indelible mark on Art as "Heroin" had, and it hardly mattered that it sounded like every other shit-kicker tune beloved by the local rednecks. What it told him was that there were no limits to creative expression when it came to songwriting, so long as the message was truthful.

Despite some membership turnover, by 1971 the Mt Lehman Grease Band had a loyal following that was helping to put them on the radar of promoters in Vancouver, leading to more substantial, yet still relatively small gigs. One memorable night occurred when they were booked into the Surrey Centennial Arts Centre along with the artist known as Valdy, at that point a regionally popular folk singer in the James Taylor mould, based near Victoria and a leading exponent of the era's "back to the land" philosophy. It was an odd pairing, to be sure, and since the show was taking place on the Mt Lehman Band's home turf, their usual rowdy fans made up most of the audience. The crowd subsequently booed Valdy mercilessly to the point where he could not perform, and police officers there to keep the peace were forced to quell a mini-riot before the Mt Lehman Band even hit the stage.

For Valdy, the experience proved so traumatic that soon afterward he put it all down on paper in the form of "Rock and Roll Song": "I came into town as a man of renown, a writer of songs about freedom and joy / A hall had been rented and I was presented as the kind of a singer that all could enjoy / As I climbed up the stair to the stage that was there / It was obvious something was missing / I could tell by the vibe they wouldn't be bribed / They weren't in the mood to listen."

"Rock and Roll Song" was released in 1972 on Valdy's debut album *Country Man*, becoming a minor radio hit thanks to the newly enacted Canadian-content broadcasting regulations, and further leading to Valdy winning a Juno Award in 1973 in the category of outstanding folk performance.

Technically, the Mt Lehman Grease Band was billed as the Shmorgs that night, one of their more colourful pseudonyms and a by-product of David Mitchell's blossoming image, enhanced by an ever-present top hat and cane, and encouraged by his partner, Marlene. "I was actually Doctor Shmorg, that was my name," Mitchell said. "I'm not sure where that came from. Art may have named me Doctor Shmorg—who knows?"

> Doctor Shmorg was very charismatic and was hard to corner if we had an above-ground show, as he was loved by all and sundry. By "above-ground," I mean the odd hall we were able to rent. Up to a thousand kids would show up from one end of the Fraser Valley to the other.

Sticking with a cartoonish name like the Shmorgs certainly seemed a more accurate reflection of Art's inherent resistance to any form of doctrine, in this case the movement toward "heavy" sounds spearheaded by bands such as Led Zeppelin and Black Sabbath that became entrenched during the first couple of years of the new decade. At the same time, the band appeared poised to get more serious about its career aspirations. For Mitchell, it was a conversation he always attempted to put off but eventually could no longer avoid.

"Art and I were living together and had quite a close relationship for a few years, so there was a shared recognition that if we kept doing this, it could become something more than a crazy avocation," Mitchell recalled. "We went through a lot of drummers and bass players, but we were starting to attract some different musicians who were a little better. That was making us better, and our following was continually growing. But with me being not much of a careerist and not a very talented musician—I was a lead singer, but I couldn't really sing, I just shouted a lot, played blues harp, and incited the audience—I wasn't really interested in doing that for the long term, so I was getting ready to move on."

> The show with Valdy was our last before Doctor Shmorg went off to university. The place was jam-packed. Mitzo pretended to die onstage and was carried off on a stretcher. Some people were actually convinced that he was dead. As we played, I could see chains glinting as they swung through the air out of the open fire exits. It was definitely not a love-in.

Mitchell began his studies at Simon Fraser University in autumn 1971, majoring in history while simultaneously stoking an interest in politics. The two eventually came together in 1983, when Mitchell published a well-regarded biography of British Columbia's longest-serving premier, W.A.C. Bennett, which led Mitchell to enter politics himself. He was elected to the BC Legislative Assembly in 1991, representing the affluent riding of West Vancouver–Garibaldi as a Liberal. Mitchell held his seat until 1996, whereupon he took a position as vice president of external relations at SFU and similar positions at the University of Ottawa and Queen's University, where his fundraising abilities led to significant growth on all three campuses. Mitchell went on to work with other non-governmental organizations, building ties among volunteer groups, governments, and the private sector, before eventually settling in Calgary and continuing his work there.

"After I started university, I still kept in touch with Art and the band, and would play with them occasionally, but I was really moving in a different direction," Mitchell said. "Art and a few of the others wanted to continue playing music, and that was great. Of that original nucleus of group members, Art was the only one who really persisted or survived. And I say 'survived' in all seriousness. There were musicians and band managers who overdosed and died, and who committed suicide. There were a lot of casualties from that period. It was pretty rough. I mean, young people back in those days were doing some pretty wild and crazy stuff, but Art always remained focused, something I've noted throughout his career. When we were together, those were the formative creative years for Art, and he emerged from that as a driving force, and people who've known him since that time, certainly myself, are really proud of him."

Mitchell's departure from the scene did effectively put an end to the original Mt Lehman Grease Band—or whatever they chose to call themselves. But in 1972, those who maintained faith in rock and roll's defining spirit, like Art, were about to be validated in a completely unexpected way and, in a sense, reborn.

CHAPTER 3

WHITE ROCK RIOT

WHEN ASKED TO NAME his life-changing gig, John Armstrong was quick to respond, "There've been several—Stones in '72 at the Coliseum, Stooges at Pender Ballroom, New York Dolls at the Commodore—but I'll say the Mt Lehman Grease Band at Maillardville Hall. This was the first time I saw Art Bergmann play, and discovered he lived just down the road from my high school. I knew immediately he'd been touched by the gods."

In 1957, the beachfront area within Surrey known as White Rock—named for a large white boulder on the shore of Semiahmoo Bay long revered by the local Indigenous community, and used by mariners as a navigation marker—voted to incorporate as its own city in response to growing anger among citizens who felt underserved by the Surrey municipal government. The separation subsequently had a major impact on the kids living near the reconstituted border, with those just on the north side, in Surrey, forced to be bused several miles each day to attend school. That geographical technicality ended up making all the difference in the lives of many teens, John Armstrong among them.

"In the summer of 1973, I got *Raw Power* by the Stooges, the first New York Dolls album, Roxy Music, T. Rex, and after that, that was all I wanted to do," he said. "I didn't care about anything else. My basketball sat abandoned in the driveway, and my comic books gathered dust. And because I had to go to school in Cloverdale, I ended up meeting some guys who were very good musicians who had a band, and I started hanging out with them—begging for lessons. That's how I met Art Bergmann, and then everything went out the window."

There had already been signs over the previous two years that a more vicious wave of youth rebellion was building in Vancouver. Mayor Tom Campbell's lack of tolerance for anti-authoritarian behaviour, led to what was called Operation Dustpan, a concerted effort to clamp down on vagrancy and anyone who dared to drink alcohol or smoke marijuana in public. When a large group gathered in Gastown in 1971 to specifically challenge Campbell's edict with a "smoke-in," police didn't hold back in dispersing the crowd with batons, and the resulting newspaper images shocked the general Vancouver population and reinforced some already stark cultural divisions. Then, in 1972, the Rolling Stones chose Vancouver to kick off their first North American tour in three years. It was an announcement that thrilled many, including Art, while putting just as many others on edge, given that the Stones' previous US jaunt had culminated in the Altamont disaster, during which a young Black man had been stabbed to death by a Hells Angel in front of the stage for reportedly pulling out a handgun.

Although the music business had learned hard lessons in crowd control from that terrible day, the Stones' return was an event that naturally attracted many segments of the population aside from those fortunate enough, like Art, to get tickets to the June 3 show at the Pacific Coliseum. Some came with no other motive than to be a part of the atmosphere outside the arena, while others turned up only to find out they had purchased counterfeit tickets from one of the scores of scalpers looking to make a fast buck. Still others, said to be members of self-styled "revolutionary" groups such as the Youngbloods and the Clark Park Gang, arrived with the sole intention of causing mayhem. As showtime approached and an estimated crowd of two thousand outside the Coliseum became increasingly unruly, police lined up in formation to prevent any forced entry. Soon, bottles—and even Molotov cocktails—started flying during a melee that left thirty officers injured and an untold number of rioters beaten with truncheons. When the show ended, Art and everyone else who had been oblivious to what had been going on outside the Coliseum opened the doors to find a sea of broken glass, charred and bloodstained concrete, and police on horseback clearing away stragglers. The following day's newspapers praised the efforts of the Vancouver police this time, with some commentators going so far as to blame the entire fracas on infiltrators from Surrey who, as some in Vancouver believed, lived by no moral code. As the arrest reports were tallied, Vancouver city council moved quickly to pass a temporary ban on rock concerts in the city, including a highly anticipated appearance by Led Zeppelin on June 18. The battle lines now seemed clearly drawn.

Still, there may have been a grain of truth in how Vancouverites perceived the Surrey contingent, given how the newly constituted Shmorgs continued to conduct their shows whenever they were allowed to play. As John Armstrong recalled, "Art just rented halls or churches, any place he could find, and put on these shows that became absolute bacchanals. There'd be bikers, leftover hippies, general sketchy people, and fresh-faced young women who had no idea about the evil nonsense they were entering into. The first one I ever went to, I walked in and the first thing I noticed were these big green plastic garbage bins with bags in them filled with liquid. I asked what was going on, and was told, 'That's Mount Lehman brew.' I said, 'What's Mount Lehman brew?' The guy said, 'Everybody just puts something in.' Someone would pour in a bottle of wine and some gin, and if somebody had some acid they'd throw that in. Everybody just dipped empty beer bottles into these garbage bins and drank this stuff all night.

"So, the first night I saw Art play, the grand finale to the night was his younger brother [Hans] onstage, naked, singing 'Jumpin' Jack Flash.' There were people fucking, there were people just sitting there communing with the universe, there were people dancing around out of their minds. I'd never seen anything like it in my life. It's the closest I think you could come to the Ken Kesey acid tests. All the laws of God and man had been suspended. So I said, 'I definitely want to be a part of this.'"

Another memorable night occurred when a plan was hatched to have the band play a birthday party for Heather Haley and fellow Mt Lehman Band/Shmorgs devotee Jim Cummins at Surrey's Elgin Hall, one of the oldest facilities of its kind in the area. It took several days to clean up the debris afterward. "Those guys played so many shows like that," Haley said. "It got to a point where somebody we knew had to rent a hall as a 'private event,' because if they said it was to put on a show by the Mt Lehman Band or the Shmorgs, the venue would just say, 'No way.'"

"We used to call them 'zoos,'" drummer Murphy Farrell explained. "It didn't matter where we played around the Lower Mainland, hordes of youth would show up because everyone knew it would be an excuse to get crazy. The 'Mount Lehman brew' thing happened one night when we set up a show at the Mount Lehman Hall, and the cops blocked off the access road. Some guys dragged these garbage cans full of dandelion wine across the fields, and people got the idea of adding whatever they'd brought with them. That kind of thing went on for a couple of years, and somehow we survived it."

> Along with bowls of peyote and gallons of dandelion wine laced with LSD,
> I remember oil-drum fires, monkey trees, and wild sexual experimentation.
> The songs were about teenage drinking and sex, but we weren't punk—just
> a bunch of noisy hippies. Those parties left a permanent impression on my
> young mind.

Art attempted to keep the party going for a time after David Mitchell left the band, knowing they could still attract significant crowds. But eventually it became necessary for practical reasons for Art to step away from the small-scale travelling circus he'd created, which now included his brother Hans, who, together with Farrell in a duo called Hans and Feet, often served as the opening act. Art found lucrative work in the isolated sawmill towns of Crescent Spur and Loos, several hundred kilometers north of Surrey, on the Fraser River near the Alberta border. There, he loaded and unloaded trains for a winter, sometimes in minus-30-degree conditions. Although the pay was sorely needed, Art's frustration overcame him one day; he pushed a load of items off a boxcar and simply walked away.

Mid-1970s, just prior to punk's arrival.
(COURTESY HEATHER HALEY)

As he made his way back south, Art's main thoughts were about forming a new version of the Shmorgs that would keep him from doing any menial work of that sort ever again, and he put the word out immediately upon his return home. Farrell was game, as was a hotshot guitarist named Peter Draper, who was dating Heather Haley. When Dennis Ingvaldson joined on bass, he recommended his sister Oleene after Art suggested adding a couple of female backup singers in order to better replicate the sound of the Rolling Stones' *Exile on Main St.* Oleene Ingvaldson had grown up with Art in Cloverdale, so joining the Shmorgs seemed more like an extension of her social life.

"I actually remember as a kid driving by Art's house on 164 Street and seeing him playing guitar out front under a tree," Oleene said. "Later, when David Mitchell left the Mt Lehman Band, Art knew I could sing, so he asked if I would join the Shmorgs. I was pregnant at the time with my first child, so I told him that I would, after I had the baby. He'd wanted to have two female backup singers in the band, but I don't think the other girl he'd asked could cut it, so it ended up just being me."

Although Ingvaldson remembered playing many wild gigs—"A lot of the guys in the Gypsy Wheelers motorcycle gang were big fans of ours, and for some reason I always felt safe when they were around"— a growing sense of the band's potential took hold as Art began reshaping his vision for the Shmorgs.

The focus on playing no-nonsense rock and roll remained, but a new twist was added after 1972, due to the impact the British glam rock movement was having everywhere. Almost overnight, David Bowie, T. Rex, and Roxy Music had made everything that came before them seem obsolete, not only through the androgynous images they projected, but also through songs that rejected rock and roll's misogynistic tendencies, as well as reality in general. It was music that pointed the way to the future, and those who chose to ignore it were doomed to be left behind.

Haley remembered, "After Bowie's *Ziggy Stardust* album came out, my friends and I sort of glommed on to it, and in some ways it helped get me through high school. The whole visual element to it was really exciting, and we all embraced it in our own ways. There was one really wild Halloween party when Art showed up with his face painted and wearing see-through tights and a long cape. I don't think he was trying to be Bowie exactly, but he really freaked everyone out. Art could pull that kind of thing off, though, just because of the way he always carried himself. I think even at that time people recognized his charisma and found him very intriguing. Some of that also had to do with Art writing his own songs, which hardly anyone did in our small town. For those of us who wanted to be artists, we all admired Art because he was actually doing it."

Haley added that Art was recognized for more than just his musical chops. He turned many heads around town after he'd saved enough money to purchase a used red Jaguar, which he often drove accompanied by his shaggy dog Bernie, who'd tear up the back seat without any fear of punishment. "After that car, Art got an old brown Mercedes," Haley said. "He and Murphy took it down to California one time. They were expecting it would die, and then I guess they were going to ditch it and then figure out a way to get back. But it ran, and they ended up scratching 'Desert Rat' into the paint on the trunk. Art brought back avocados, and that was the first time I'd ever seen one. So yeah, Art was kind of a local celebrity, even in high school."

That simple act of trying to create an identity did indeed fly in the face of accepted norms, as John Armstrong concurred. "What was notable about the Shmorgs was they did mostly original songs. In the early '70s, there was a club-band world where you just got a list from your management—'Learn these songs by next week and put them in the set.' You were just a human jukebox, and that was the only work you could get in nightclubs. You literally could not work in a club otherwise. Bands would try to sneak songs in that they had written and say they were by somebody else, and would get in big trouble for that."

Farrell now admits that the Shmorgs played by those rules whenever it was necessary to land well-paying, week-long runs, but Art's vision for the band was always to play his original material. "Art wrote based on his own experiences," Farrell said. "In fact, one of the songs I remember we did was called 'Going Back to Loos,' which came out of his time working up there. I think he got a lot of that from his father, who was really supportive. We could rehearse in the basement of their house, and he helped us build a little recording space. After Frank retired, he started writing a lot more himself for newspapers and magazines. He was a free thinker and had this attitude of 'If you've got something to say, say it.' That really became Art's credo too."

However, such stridency was mixed with a wicked sense of humour, especially in situations where others attempted to dictate the direction the Shmorgs should be taking. Glam rock may have been the rage in Vancouver, but it didn't register with much of the band's audience. It was also the era of slick, LA–produced rock epitomized by the Eagles, Linda Ronstadt, and Fleetwood Mac, which the Shmorgs attempted to resist through sometimes not-so-subtle mockery. Farrell said, "I think today, some of the stuff we did could be called roots rock, but for the most part it was tongue-in-cheek. There was one song Art wrote called 'Cheese Deluxe' that was a total country-and-western send-up, and everyone saw it for the joke it was."

> I laboured at all kinds of jobs in between gigs, even as a subcontractor at the Langley post office with this guy who was notorious for driving a van with no brakes. That was actually fun for a while. My songs sucked after the crudities of the teenage years, I don't know why. I went from dirty Dadaism to floundering and back out again. We played tons of garage, R&B, and rockabilly covers as well. I just hadn't studied enough art history. Murphy and I stumbled around every bar in British Columbia for a while, getting fired for not playing covers. We sold drugs at schools to pay our way around. Playing my bent half-hour epics, we met some cool people until we heard of the great goings-on in Vancouver.

By 1975, the Shmorgs were landing regular gigs at Vancouver's Pender Auditorium and Commodore Ballroom, and the idea of doing some professional recordings increasingly seemed an attainable goal. "Our guitar player, Pete Draper, was really into recording," Farrell recalled, "so at one point we went over to Victoria, where he was living with Heather Haley, and we recorded some stuff at his house." With those tapes in hand, the Shmorgs seemed ready to take the next step, even though their options remained limited.

> I remember approaching a couple of B-room bookers in Vancouver. My life at that time was a series of confused run-ins with some of the worst hotel pub bookers and owners all over BC.

The biggest hurdle for the Shmorgs seemed to be their name, which consistently caused their business connections to question their ultimate goals. As Oleene Ingvaldson recalled, "Both Art and Murphy were adamant that we keep it 'the Shmorgs.' Their argument was, 'Everybody wants to be part of Shmorg-ology.' I remember getting into an argument with both of them over that."

The bad feelings lingered within Ingvaldson, and her own interest in being part of Shmorg-ology would effectively end not long after. "I do remember Art telling me that this was the first band he'd been in that he felt could really do something, and it was true that we were really good. So that's probably what made me most angry over them refusing to change the name. Looking back, I kind of regret that."

> The whole Shmorgs thing was silly—"Shmorg-ology" indeed. We were ass-holes about it, no doubt there. But Oleene's husband at the time hated us for trying to steal his bride. Murphy and I were both in love with her. Doing the Shmorgs without the Doctor was a hopeless case. We were almost backwoods and I had no education regarding the urban squalor I thirsted for when I heard Lou Reed. My songwriting was all over the map.

Pre-punk lineup of the Shmorgs, with Oleene Ingvaldson on backing vocals. (COURTESY OLEENE INGVALDSON)

The Shmorgs forged ahead into 1977, whereupon they secured the financial backing of a friend, Brent Johnston, to make an album. The band set up at a studio called Sonic Lab, run by Simon "Si" Garber (later known as the long-time sound engineer for the Vancouver Folk Music Festival), and proceeded to cut eight of Art's original songs, several of which were co-written with two members of the White Rock crew, Jim Cummins and Bill Scherk, with the latter also providing the Surrealist-inspired painting that adorned the eventual album cover. The final results were a pale representation of the live shows the Shmorgs were known for, and with the songs themselves, Art seemed caught in a creative bind between attempting to make meaningful statements, as on tracks like "Exhortation Rag," and offering pure rock and roll fluff with "So Ya Wanna Be a Shmorg" and others.

> I was trying to progress beyond just doing basic three-chord rock and roll, but at that point I was still learning how to write songs. We went through a bunch of lineups, and I ended up doing all the writing for the band, which was a real burden. The Shmorgs album was very misdirected the way it was produced.

Without any connections to retail distribution, band members issued promissory notes to friends and fans and personally delivered copies of *Shmorgs* once it was pressed in the summer of 1978 under the band's ad hoc label Stray Records, derived from one of its more cohesive tracks, "Stray Ravers." By then, however, it was all but impossible to ignore the latest sounds coming from New York, London, and, to a lesser extent, closer to home in LA and San Francisco. What was being called punk rock had taken the glam aesthetic and reconnected it to the harsh realities of street life and teenage anger given voice in the songs of Lou Reed and the music of the Stooges and MC5.

> The mid-'70s was an awful time and I hated all the bands. In '76, John Armstrong gave me a Sex Pistols cassette he'd picked up from someone in England, and then I heard Television's *Marquee Moon*. In between those two poles, I deconstructed everything and started over. I'd heard "Heroin" when I was sixteen but I didn't understand it. It sort of laid there in my subconscious until those early shows in Vancouver, when it felt like there were all these voices in the dark going, "You can scream as loud as you want, you can say anything you want, you can do whatever you feel like."

The first bands in Vancouver that formed out of this cultural morass were the Furies—whose drummer, Jim Walker, would soon seek the source in London and wind up co-founding John Lydon's post–Sex Pistols band Public Image Ltd.—and the Dishrags, formed by three female, Ramones-loving high-school students from Victoria.

Art's younger friends from White Rock, John Armstrong, Bill Scherk, and Gord Nicholl, were also getting in on the action by forming their own band, the Shits, and on August 16,

1977, the day Elvis Presley shuffled off this mortal coil while on his toilet seat in Graceland, the sound of primal rock and roll echoed around Semiahmoo Bay from the White Rock bandshell, as the Shmorgs and the Shits played alongside a recently formed Vancouver band called the Skulls, whose lineup included guitarist Joe "Shithead" Keithley, bassist Brian "Wimpy Roy" Goble, and drummer Ken "Dimwit" Montgomery.

> We were friends with the infamous Mud Bay Slim, who got the job booking bands at the bandshell in White Rock. He hired the Shits and the Skulls. The Skulls came with their coterie of fans to this innocent little bandshell and nobody knew what to think. It went okay for a while, but then they started playing "Anarchy in the UK" and Armstrong got in a scuffle with their singer, this little guy. We knew the words and chords inside out, and [John] didn't think the singer was performing very well. There was a little bit of a punch-up, and we were all throwing shit at them. I'd already played with the Amazing Shits earlier that afternoon [on bass], and let's just say that punk doesn't look very good in the daylight. Bill Scherk fired at the audience with a starter's pistol. Nobody knew what the fuck was going on, and I'm amazed the crowd didn't trample each other trying to get away. It was nuts.

According to Scherk, "Art played bass for us that day with a bag over his head. We drank two bottles of Jack Daniel's over the course of a six-song set. I don't think any public performance has ever contained that much cursing. It was Simon Wilde [later bassist for Rabid] who fired the starter's pistol. We all moved to the Shmorgs' rundown farmhouse within a few months, and everything in that place was about art and music. And maybe drinking."

The day after the show, Keithley had the presence of mind to call Tom Harrison, music critic for Vancouver's alternative weekly newspaper, the *Georgia Straight*, and described what had gone down. Harrison in turn devoted a significant portion of his music-notes column that week to the "White Rock riot," and deemed the Skulls, "Vancouver's most hated band." It was the first indication of what was to come, and by the start of 1978 punk had fully taken root in Vancouver. The scene boasted its own fanzine, *Snot Rag*, while the Skulls split off into two new bands, the Keithley-led D.O.A. and the Subhumans. The Shits had assumed the more palatable name the Monitors without making any musical concessions, and the Shmorgs, it seemed, were caught up in all of it simply through their affiliations. For Art, it meant finally abandoning any plans of "making it" in the traditional music-business sense, especially when faced with how Vancouver clubs were openly conspiring to suppress the new bands.

They instead found unlikely homes in venues like the Japanese Hall, where the Furies and the Dishrags put on the first local punk show on July 30, 1977. D.O.A. debuted there on February 20, 1978, and on March 17, the Shmorgs and the Monitors threw their own punk rock coming-out party at the Japanese Hall, billed as the "Vancouver invasion" of the White Rock scene. In early September, D.O.A. was back in White Rock opening for the Shmorgs, and by then Art could no longer avoid the stark choice of where to put his musical allegiance.

"It was a funny time in Vancouver then because we were really eager to play, but then the scene changed," Farrell recalled. "The gig we did at Semiahmoo Bay with the Skulls was really the turning point, because after that I could tell Art wanted to go his own way. We had some pretty hardcore tunes, but as a band I don't think we were equipped to fit in with what the punk bands were doing. I had a job then too, and Art wanted to move to Vancouver with some of the other White Rock guys, so I wasn't about to stand in his way. But we've always had that family connection, and that's something that kept us close ever since."

I'd been fired from so many bars for playing my own music. In those days, we'd drive 500 miles for a week-long gig and get fired after Monday night, and have no money to get back home. One place we got fired from in Merritt had fired the Skulls the week before—they had thrown the shrubbery into the pool. Playing Lillooet on a Saturday night with John Armstrong and Bill Scherk as guests is a fond memory. The white greasers hated us, but the Indigenous residents loved us.

Murphy had bought an old police van for our gear, which included a PA system that we made a little money from by renting it out to the new bands. I remember visiting Oleene when I drove by her place on Vancouver Island on my way to set up our PA for the San Francisco band the Readymades, who were playing in Victoria. I had [future environmental activist and artist] Soledad Reeve with me, and we both had wild, butch hair. Oleene bid us adieu with "Go run off with your new punk friends, Art."

House party, late 1970s.
(COURTESY HEATHER HALEY)

I FELL IN LOVE
WITH THE ENEMY

As Art gave more indication that he was ready to move on from the Shmorgs, guitarist Peter Draper and Heather Haley decided to seek out new opportunities in Alberta. But before moving there they rented a house in Surrey near Princess Margaret Secondary School for several months in 1976 and 1977. With Art in need of accommodation at that moment, they gladly offered some space and were soon intimately acquainted with his new, close circle of young friends.

"That was when I met John Armstrong and Bill Scherk for the first time, and I think they were still teenagers then," Haley said. "John especially was there a lot just because he wanted to be around Art. He'd skip school and he and I would drink tea in the afternoon together. But one day I remember Peter and Art and I had gone out and when we came back John and Bill were there. Somehow, they'd managed to get a hold of a cello from band class or somewhere and had chopped it into little pieces on the living room floor. They were both drunk and stoned, and I was pretty mad at them for making such a huge mess. But I guess I can see it now as a harbinger of things to come."

Scherk recalled, "Our friend Gord Nicholl had a teeny little apartment in a building that has long been demolished, so Armstrong and I rented an apartment there as well. Just a three-minute walk down Marine Drive in White Rock was the Beach Aps, or Beach Apartments, where Art Bergmann and a circulating tableau of musicians, including the remnants of the Shmorgs and what would have been considered the alt-rock community, congregated to make noise. I think the impetus came when we heard something out of the UK. I don't remember who it was, maybe the Damned, but the notion was that anyone can play, anyone can write, and anyone can perform. So the step from 'Hey, I wrote a song' to 'Hey, do you want to write a song with me?' to 'Hey, let's get drunk' followed very naturally and rolled like a snowball down a very steep hill."

Armstrong now admits that he was essentially at Art's beck and call then, eager to do anything from moving gear and stringing guitars to going on beer runs, just so Art would teach him everything he knew about music and playing guitar. "Art was really well versed, and he was an exceptional guitar player," Armstrong said. "He was a great teacher, and God love him that he put up with me, because I must have been such an enormous pain in the ass. I just attached myself to him and wouldn't leave until I learned how to play the guitar. So I guess it was in his own best interest that he taught me—it was the only way he was going to get rid of me."

Although the Shmorgs remained a going concern, Armstrong recognized the sea change in Art beginning to occur in the summer of 1976, after he shared the cassette of yet-to-be-released Sex Pistols recordings. This, combined with the Stooges and the New York Dolls being constantly on the turntable at the house, kept widening the already growing gulf between Art and the rest of the Shmorgs.

> My repertoire became much more pointed after I heard the Sex Pistols in '76. I was very critical of everything I wrote, but all my self-doubt went out the window after that. You could say what you wanted to say, and you could say it loud and clear. Everything was different.

It seemed he passed the point of no return after Armstrong, Scherk, and Nicholl formed the Shits in the summer of 1977 and Art regularly joined them on bus trips into Vancouver to check out the new bands. By the time the Shmorgs had their last hurrah at the Japanese Hall in March 1978, it was a foregone conclusion that relocating to the city was Art's most practical and creatively stimulating option. He first found a residence at 509 East Cordova, a space that would soon become one of the Vancouver punk community's important social hubs and places of refuge, given that anyone who had suddenly bucked the accepted rock and roll uniform of long hair and flared denim was immediately under suspicion. Armstrong recalls the most violent incident occurring after he, Art, and some others had gone to see a show by Detroit garage-rock pioneer Mitch Ryder. "This car stops and these guys leap out. At least one of them had a tire iron and they're screaming, 'Fuckin' fags!' We're like, 'No, we're just innocent punk rockers!' But we looked the same—short hair, straight-leg pants, fancy clothes, and that was enough. If we weren't fags, we were the next best thing, and so they beat the hell out of all of us. After a while, that kind of thing abated, but there was enormous resistance at first."

> We'd all take the bus into Vancouver from White Rock, but we'd miss the last bus home and scuz around all night getting into trouble. That went on for a while, and I had all sorts of shitty jobs in White Rock, but then I some-how moved to the city in 1978 and got welfare. [Future D.O.A. guitarist] Dave Gregg's girlfriend Cathy Cleghorn found us the little shack in Japan-town that we called 509. I lived there with John Armstrong and Bill Scherk. We shopped in thrift stores and ate bean deluxe. The Shmorgs were almost done by then. We were replacing guitar players and didn't have any real songwriting focus. By then, punk rock was very much upon us.
>
> There used to be guys who would drive around in cars and queer-bash on the West End. We were still new to the city then, and we were oblivious

to it. These guys came racing past us and just about ran us over, and of course we yelled out, "You fucking cunts!" They came back around the next block and beat the shit out of us with crowbars and tire irons. I ended up with a broken jaw and a lesson not to go to any more Mitch Ryder shows.

The run of events at the Japanese Hall, which had been organized by upstart promoters Ross Drummond and Kat Hammond, came to an end in April 1978, after a double bill of D.O.A. and San Francisco's Avengers resulted in serious damage to the building. Nevertheless, the seeds planted there had firmly taken hold and the music was too prevalent to ignore by that summer. The *Georgia Straight* was the first significant media outlet to take up the cause, inviting some of the punks to participate in a "battle of the bands" held on June 23 at a dance club on Hornby Street called the Body Shop. D.O.A.—just about to release its debut four-song EP *Disco Sucks* on its own Sudden Death label—received no votes from the judges. Ten days later, on Canada Day, Joe Keithley and company headlined a free concert in Stanley Park, with a lineup that also included the Subhumans, which, along with his former Skulls rhythm section of "Wimpy Roy" Goble and "Dimwit" Montgomery, featured bassist Gerry "Useless" Hannah, who would achieve further infamy a few years later, after leaving the band to co-found the revolutionary group Direct Action, also known as the Squamish Five.

In July, as well, a Surrey band called No Fun released its debut independent 7-inch EP, *Fall for a Cliché*, and new bands the Pointed Sticks and Rabid made their public debuts in August at the Quadra Club, a lesbian disco formerly known as Lucy's. That month also saw Ted Thomas and Gerry Barad of Kitsilano record store Quintessence—where the latest international punk releases were guaranteed to be in stock—make the jump into releasing music themselves with Tim Ray & A.V.'s *A.V.E.P.* 7-inch. Before the end of the year, Quintessence Records would be a full-fledged label after putting out D.O.A.'s single "The Prisoner" and the Pointed Sticks' vinyl debut, "What Do You Want Me to Do?"

Meanwhile, in autumn 1978, John Armstrong and Bill Scherk (now known, respectively, by their new punk monikers Buck Cherry and Bill Shirt), along with Gord Nicholl on keyboards, reconfigured the Monitors with guitarist Terry Bowes, bassist Ross Carpenter, and drummer Robert Bruce, first taking the name Frantic Technicians before settling on Active Dog. With Armstrong's lead guitar and Scherk's lead vocals providing a formidable front line, the band quickly marked its territory and rose up the Vancouver punk pecking order. Still, there was one crucial voice yet to be heard from.

All of the activity occurring around him naturally fuelled Art's ambition, and despite being kept on the sidelines by his injuries from the beating, he channelled his rage into a new cache of material. While unable to sing because of the broken jaw, he participated in the action by filling the Monitors' need of a bass player for a good portion of 1978. However, it was understood that his place in that band was merely a temporary arrangement until he could plant his flag with a band of his own.

The lag time may have been beneficial to Art in some ways, since it took the mainstream Vancouver media nearly until the end of the year to start seriously covering the punk scene.

The catalyst was budding journalist Les Wiseman's feature article "Punks on Parade" in the September 1978 issue of *Vancouver* magazine, accompanied by a hilariously posed cover photo of the Subhumans' "Wimpy Roy" Goble done up in full King's Road punk gear, antagonizing a conservatively dressed woman portrayed by his sister Deb. The magazine soon gave Wiseman his own column, "In One Ear," to keep readers fully engaged with the new music. Later in 1979, the *Georgia Straight*'s Tom Harrison was taken on by the Vancouver *Province* and henceforth became the punk community's conduit to one of the city's major daily newspapers, just as a new punk-focused tabloid, *Public Enemy*, launched its year-long run.

The scene was fully galvanized as soon as the calendar turned over to 1979, when Blondie played the Commodore Ballroom on January 2, followed by the Ramones on January 6 and Devo on January 12. However, the Commodore gig no one was going to miss was set for January 31, when the Clash would make its North American live debut. The band had just released its first official North American album, *Give 'Em Enough Rope* (the self-titled first album was still only available as an import), and had arrived in Vancouver a few days before the show. By all accounts, the quartet immediately ingratiated themselves with the local punk community, dropping into the Windmill on Granville Street—opened in autumn 1978 following the Quadra Club's closure—to see Rabid and taking part in a pickup soccer game with local luminaries in McBride Park. They also insisted on adding the Dishrags to the bill at the Commodore, alongside the scheduled opener, rock and roll legend Bo Diddley. The Clash further surprised everyone by showing up at an after-party at 509 Cordova, where they proceeded—in Art's recollection—to steal everyone's girlfriends for the night and do all the cocaine that was available. As the party raged on into the early morning, a neighbour finally called the police and a quick-thinking party attendee managed to hustle the Clash out the back door before an ugly incident ensued.

In the end, those few whirlwind days established a lasting bond between the Clash and Vancouver while emboldening everyone in the punk community. Joe Keithley later told the *Vancouver Sun*, "It kinda was the show that really opened up the scene. It was tremendous. [The Clash] were at their peak in those days. It was a total event. Everybody who could be there and was vaguely connected with the scene made sure they were there—in whatever they could do with their jacket or hair." For Art, it all provided more fuel for him to make a grand entrance once he'd found the right co-conspirators.

Jim Bescott's history in Vancouver was almost as chequered as Art's pre-punk resumé, starting with an attempt at joining the singer-songwriter ranks during the early 1970s. Bescott had been born in San Francisco in 1953 but had moved with his family to Vancouver when he was fourteen, just as the Summer of Love was in full swing. He graduated from Kitsilano Secondary School, and his musical dexterity soon found him joining a band called Riff Raff, which sold itself on the basis of being able to perform four distinct sets of music a night—vintage rock and roll, British Invasion rock, psychedelic rock, and glam rock—complete with costume changes. He later became part of a similarly unwieldy project called the Band of Love Angels, a thirteen-piece hippie collective that played largely improvised music on a variety of instruments. In the mid-'70s, Bescott enrolled at the Vancouver School of Art to develop his interest in animation, and in 1977 one of his creations was honoured at the Canadian Student Film Festival in Montreal.

However, by the following year he was caught up in the energy of the punk scene and began looking for a way in. Someone inevitably suggested that Bescott introduce himself to Art, still in the process of writing new material, and the two hit it off based on their common musical interests. Bescott was soon regularly meeting with Art at his new home base, one of a handful of row houses on the 500 block of Victoria Drive, known as Vic Row, where many other Vancouver punk-scene figures had migrated. With Bescott contributing his own ideas on bass, along with an overall enthusiasm, it became obvious that the pair was laying a solid foundation for a new band. All they needed was a drummer who could match the power and speed of Jim Walker, D.O.A.'s Chuck Biscuits, and the Subhumans' Dimwit.

Like Art and Bescott, Barry Taylor possessed a skill set uncommon to most punk musicians, honed through playing with a series of early '70s experimental bands and a love of jazz fusion and avant-garde music. In fact, Taylor had never really listened to any punk rock or new wave prior to putting up a "drummer available" flyer at Vancouver's Long & McQuade music store. "At the time, I had just moved to Vancouver with my wife and young child and was looking for people to play with," Taylor said. "Punk was what was happening, and I started really paying attention after seeing the [1978] Canada Day show in Stanley Park. So when I first got a call from Jim, we had a nice chat about what he and Art were doing. Then Art called me and we had a nice chat. He asked if I knew who the Ramones were, and I said yes, so I passed that test. Then he told me to bring my snare drum to this little art gallery in Gastown called Gambado's, where they had been rehearsing."

Taylor learned later that Art and Bescott had auditioned several other drummers, but upon Taylor's arrival they all three felt an instant connection that stemmed from being drawn into punk from unlikely sources. Taylor also stood out because of his bald head, the result of a childhood accident that had burned off most of his hair. "I sensed at that first meeting they had a plan to test me," he added. "They were saying, 'Well, we don't really have anything prepared,' and then Art quickly counted off '1, 2, 3, 4!' to catch me off-guard. I said, 'Whoa, let's try that again.' So I nailed the beat the second time, and after we finished the song we all looked at each other and said, 'That was pretty cool.' I soon realized that Art and Jim had a shared musical vocabulary that was much broader than what other punk musicians had, as far as I could tell, and that mixed well with my ability to play fast in odd time signatures. Somehow, that all seemed to fit within a punk rock context."

It was Bescott who suggested naming the band the K-Tels, after the company known for marketing unusual household products such as the Veg-o-Matic food slicer and the Feather Touch Knife. By the late '70s, through its Canadian headquarters in Winnipeg, K-Tel had become ubiquitous with its gaudy compilation albums of popular hits, made through direct negotiations for reproduction rights with labels and artists. Although calling themselves the K-Tels mocked the perception of punks as amateurs only in it to make a fast buck, the irony was that everyone considered the trio the most musically accomplished band in the scene right from the outset.

The K-Tels: Art, Jim Bescott, Barry Taylor. (ALEX WATERHOUSE-HAYWARD)

> I met Jim Bescott at a Shmorgs show in Vancouver in early 1978. The rest
> of the band didn't want to follow me down the rabbit hole to the wild life in
> Vancouver, so I decided to start the band that became the K-Tels. Jim was
> such an amazing player, and he encouraged me to let loose on the guitar. I
> sort of tore apart everything I knew and then fully added it back again into
> the new frenetic style of playing.

The K-Tels made their live debut in early 1979 at a jam-packed Gambado's, not long after cobbling together a short, blindingly explosive set divided between Art and Bescott's originals, such as "Son of Spam," and covers of '60s garage rock nuggets they all loved, like the Electric Prunes' "I Had Too Much to Dream (Last Night)." But it wasn't until February 16, 1979, that the K-Tels solidified their status with an unbilled appearance at a show dubbed "the St. Valentine's Day Massacre Dance" at O'Hara's, a former CN steamship terminal turned rock club on Main Street. Headlined by the Pointed Sticks, the Subhumans, and the Dishrags, the K-Tels were only allotted a few songs, meaning they avoided the confrontation between punks and bikers later on in the night that resulted in several people being taken to hospital.

Taylor recalled, "I was sitting at home with my wife and kid when Jim called and asked if I wanted to do this gig that night. I said, 'Uh, okay,' and piled my drums into my car and drove down there. It turned out to be a pretty crazy scene, but really exciting. I remember there were beer cans flying everywhere as we were playing."

A couple of weeks later, the K-Tels were back in the more familiar confines of Gambado's, where Les Wiseman saw them for the first time. "It was a small place with a low stage," he said. "I think the Dishrags also played, and thirty people in there made it feel like a sardine can. Art was wearing glasses, which was unusual to start with, but I also couldn't help noticing his guitar, this beat up old Stratocaster with the strings an inch above the frets. But he played it incredibly and the songs were all instantly memorable. From the minute I heard 'I Hate Music,' I was hooked."

> Interview with *Snot Rag*, March 29, 1979:
> **Q:** What's the influence in your music? Like to me, I get a kind of psyche-
> delic '60s, definitely '60s, influence.
> **Art:** I'd never admit to that. Influences? D.O.A., Pointed Sticks, John Arm-
> strong, Bill Shirt, Active Dog, Dishrags—those are mine. You see, I'd heard
> all the local bands first, before I'd heard most of the stuff from the States.
>
> I never played commercial music at all—I only wanted to play original
> stuff. I was just out in the country for too long, you know, too laid-back out
> there. Everybody keeps telling me how big of a thing [new wave] is going to
> be and you've got to jump on this new-wave bandwagon.

With authorities putting O'Hara's under scrutiny following the St. Valentine's Massacre show, and the Windmill ceasing its run of shows, bands once again started scrambling for places to play. Bescott, who had willingly taken on the role of the K-Tels' chief organizer, suggested as a solution the Smilin' Buddha Cabaret, a dilapidated bar at 109 East Hastings that had originally opened in 1952 as an upscale dinner dance club.

In 1962 Lachman and Nancy Jir purchased it, turning it into a venue for burlesque performers and both local and international R&B acts, the former including future comedy star Tommy Chong's band the Shades. Lachman Jir established his own legend around the same time, after apparently ejecting a pre-fame Jimi Hendrix for playing too loud. But by 1979, the Smilin' Buddha was just another glaring symbol of the Downtown Eastside's descent into a haven for hard drugs and prostitution—in other words, the perfect spot for the city's new punk rock headquarters. The K-Tels played the first punk show there on March 24, and most of the other bands in town followed suit thereafter.

> Jim was a denizen of all the old bars, and actually played in them. He knew Lachman and asked if we could play there. He managed to book us for a week, even though [Jir] shut us down the first night for being too loud. The Subhumans played the next week, and D.O.A. the week after that. But really there was nothing good about the Buddha. It was the only place to play, and it stunk to high heaven from fifty-year-old grease in the kitchen.

Jir seemed happy to have the influx of new business and paid little attention to the rules when it came to underage patrons. Tracy Brooks, later the singer for the Hip Type, would often find her way inside by paying the cover charge with a roll of nickels. "It was like a clubhouse," she described. "You knew everybody that was there, and if you didn't, you found out who they were pretty fast." Brooks added that kids who couldn't afford entry nonetheless hung out in the club's back alley, just to be as close to the action as they could. "That's where the police would come. They would confiscate belts, they would confiscate wristbands, they would confiscate your dog collar if you were wearing one. They would confiscate anything. And boy oh boy, God help you if you got caught with a beer."

In full flight at the Smilin' Buddha Cabaret. (ALEX WATERHOUSE-HAYWARD)

Jir eventually devised his own strategies to deal with the underage crowd, as Vancouver punk historian Scott Beadle explained. "If police were around, Lachman would come running out and herd us all into the kitchen—which was also the band room—and lock the door. If the cops came in and he was more nervous than usual, we got used to the drill of going through the trap door in the kitchen down into the beer cellar. He'd lift it open and be like, 'Go in, go in!'"

As word spread of the scene developing at the Smilin' Buddha, pressure mounted on the police to suppress it. It came to a head in May 1979 at a Subhumans show, when a violent incident erupted between officers and audience members after someone incited a chant of "Kill pigs!" That was enough reason for the cops to dole out beatings and drunk-and-disorderly charges in equal measure, making it a newsworthy event. One of those caught in the fracas was Joe Keithley, who appeared on a local current-events television show the following day displaying his bruises and urging an internal investigation. For his part, Jir was brought before city council for a hearing to determine the fate of his liquor licence and faced the wrath of several councillors who regarded punk rock as, in the words of one, "on the fringe of civilization." Jir's lawyer instead claimed it was premeditated police intimidation that was to blame, and while Jir ended up keeping his licence, with each ensuing infraction the city reduced the Smilin' Buddha's official capacity.

The chaos inherent to punk rock shows was nothing new to Art, apart from the obvious us-versus-them mentality at its core. In many ways, it reflected his own belief system and ratcheted up the intensity of his onstage performances and the messages in his songs, which were now starting to flow out of him at will. In the aftermath of the Smilin' Buddha incident, he penned "No Escape," which brilliantly encapsulated the growing tensions with the police: "Who's always there when the fun begins / The music's loud they walk right in / No escape from the city police / They shut you down, you run to the streets / This town's frustrations are scrawled all over these walls / It's a new minority and how does it feel to be so small?"

Musically, "No Escape" was delivered in a tight, fast, and thoroughly catchy package that clearly hinted at the K-Tels' commercial potential. That further came into focus in June when they took the honours at the *Georgia Straight*'s now-annual Battle of the Bands, following a blistering set at the event held at Gary Taylor's Rock Room on Hornby Street. The trio played their most finely honed originals to that point: "Automan," "Where Are You" and "Don't Tell Me," as if daring the judges to vote against them.

"I hate to describe it this way, but I do think our songs were a couple of notches above everyone else's," Barry Taylor said. "They weren't hardcore punk and they weren't new wave. They were somewhere in between, which was different at that time, and people recognized that. Once I joined, I think that took some pressure off Art and Jim and allowed them to really concentrate on songwriting, and with Art especially, he could get an idea and come back twenty minutes later with something fully formed."

ooooo

Although more bands were starting to find ways to record and release their music, the Vancouver scene was still not well documented after eighteen months. Grant McDonagh, a Quintessence

K-Tels gig posters.

employee and co-creator of *Snot Rag* with his sister Lynn, had been trying to change that as early as autumn 1978, after hitting on the idea of making a flexi-disc sampler EP for a future issue of the zine. The project soon expanded to a full-length compilation album, and a couple of fundraising concerts over the next several months helped pay for recording sessions at Sabre Sound, a basement studio run by local CBC sound engineer Chris Cutress, who agreed to release the album on his Pinned Records label. The project was close to completion by the time of the K-Tels' arrival, but the intrepid Jim Bescott managed to secure the band a place on the record not long before its final track list was determined in summer 1979. However, they had to capture something on their own, which led to a hastily arranged session with Robin Spurgin—who had been recording Vancouver bands since the early '60s—at his Psi-Chord studio. The band managed to blaze through five songs, including the one ultimately chosen for the compilation, "I Hate Music."

With its provocative title once again playing up punk stereotypes, like "No Escape" the song itself turned the tables with its razor-sharp arrangement, while Art's cynicism suggested that hate for music could turn to love pretty quickly if people actually started buying what the punks were selling. *Vancouver Complication* was released in August, with "I Hate Music" included alongside tracks from D.O.A., the Subhumans, the Pointed Sticks, Active Dog, and the Dishrags, along with some bands that could be labelled with the still relatively novel "post-punk" tag, such as U-J3RK5, formed by visual artists Ian Wallace, Jeff Wall, and Rodney Graham. As the first project of its kind in Canada, *Vancouver Complication* made a strong argument that the west coast was far outpacing the nascent independent music scenes in the country's other major urban centres, Toronto and Montreal. And with the K-Tels' participation generating their first experience in a professional recording studio, it seemed they and others were hungry for more. One of those people was Ted Thomas from Quintessence, who one day met up with the band at its rehearsal space, and left with an agreement to release a 7-inch. With the Psi-Chord sessions from which to draw, they chose "Automan" as the A-side and squeezed "Don't Tell Me" and "Where Are You?" onto the B-side. The label bore the curious credit "—Tels" out of fear of reprisal from the K-Tel corporation, something that indeed occurred before the end of the summer.

As the band came offstage after a sweat-drenched performance for an appreciative crowd on the Simon Fraser University campus, they were handed legal documents by two people whose only words were "Here, you've been served." After gathering themselves and changing clothes, the band got the gist that K-Tel was suing them for $50,000 for besmirching its name. Although the threat was real, the biggest question for the band was whether they were prepared to fight it. Fortunately, some of the other bands in town had already been receiving legal advice from a sympathetic local lawyer, who was willing to help out the K-Tels as well.

"What was interesting at that time was that you never knew who was on the fringes of the scene," Taylor said. "You obviously knew the hardcore kids by the way they dressed in public, but there were also lots of other people with high-profile jobs who would put on their leather at night and go out to the clubs. We were introduced to a lawyer who was one of these people, and he laid it all out for us that we could probably win the suit, but it would take a couple of years and cost a ton of money. So a meeting was set up and K-Tel flew out their lawyers from Winnipeg. The three of us were there and we made a deal to change our name in exchange for the lawsuit being dropped. The funniest part about it was after we signed the papers our lawyer drove K-Tel's lawyers to the airport. He had the UBC station CITR on the radio and an ad came on for our next show there at the Student Union Building—'This Saturday, don't miss the K-Tels!' I thought that was a pretty appropriate send-off."

Art was quick to wring every drop of mock persecution from the incident, saying that the lawsuit was an affront to three upstanding young Canadians. From then on, the band would be known as the Young Canadians.

With the lawsuit behind them by autumn 1979, the trio took up Ted Thomas and Gerry Barad's offer to record a new EP for Quintessence. On top of the $1,000 they'd earned from winning the *Georgia Straight*'s Battle of the Bands, they were given financial support by Gary Taylor—he of Gary Taylor's Rock Room—who had become an ardent fan of the band. It allowed them to book time at Little Mountain Sound with its fledgling house engineer Bob Rock, who had been itching to work with many of the Vancouver punk bands. Born in Winnipeg in 1954, Rock (his actual family name) moved to Victoria when he was fourteen and within a few years had formed a tight friendship with Paul Hyde, whose family had recently immigrated from England. Together, they harboured dreams of becoming rock stars, and

Following this 1979 gig, the K-Tels were forced to change their name.

The newly christened Young Canadians on the bill with the Dead Kennedys at Vancouver's Legion Hall.

upon completing high school in 1972 they both eagerly flew to the UK to see if it was possible. It was the height of glam rock, and the pair soaked it all in until they ran out of money and returned to Canada.

Over the next couple of years, Rock grew obsessed with how those records were made, and in particular with the sound of David Bowie's guitarist, Mick Ronson, who became the model for his own guitar style. But as Rock cut his teeth playing with a host of bar bands, his future suddenly came into focus in 1976 when he heard a radio ad for a six-week recording course in Vancouver. After securing a promise from his parents to pay for it, Rock took to the studio environment like a second home and immediately parlayed the experience into an entry level job at Little Mountain Sound, Vancouver's state-of-the-art recording facility.

He came under the wing of producer Bruce Fairbairn, who had made Little Mountain the headquarters for projects such as the prog-rock band Prism, whose self-titled 1977 debut album attained platinum status in Canada on the strength of the hit single "Spaceship Superstar." Although Rock gladly absorbed everything he could learn from Fairbairn, he felt more of an affinity with the Vancouver punk bands, and in 1978 he and Paul Hyde joined the fray by forming the Payola$, releasing their debut single, "China Boys" b/w "Make Some Noise," the following year on their own Slophouse label. Of course, having access to Little Mountain Sound was the pair's biggest advantage, but Rock was generous in arranging to help out other bands in the scene however he could. This most often meant setting up middle-of-the-night sessions when the studio was technically closed.

"I wanted to record and produce the bands nobody else wanted to work with at that time," Rock said. "I was just starting to figure out how to put songs and records together, but on top of that the punk era in Vancouver allowed me to be a part of something. It gave me an opportunity to be me, because by then I'd realized I was never going to be as good of a guitar player as my idols. Working with bands like the Subhumans, Pointed Sticks, and the Young Canadians was how I really learned how to make records. My fellow engineer at Little Mountain, Ron Obvious, and I would go out to the clubs together and basically decide which bands we wanted to produce and then just let them know they had an open invitation."

Given the time and money constraints, Art, Jim, and Barry came prepared to record just four songs, two per side on the eventual EP. "No Escape" was mandatory, and it was joined by "Well, Well, Well," Art's pronouncement on those who dedicated their lives to climbing the corporate ladder, and "Hullabaloo Girls," a tribute to the '60s music television program, sung by Bescott. But the song that managed to stand out from the others was "Hawaii," a snotty comment on anyone who devoted much of their year's earnings to vacation getaways. As another song with a pop-inspired arrangement, coupled with the liberal use of "fuckin'" throughout, "Hawaii" became an instant fan favourite, which Art exploited by often wearing Hawaiian shirts onstage in defiance of punk fashion etiquette. However, the song's popularity didn't sit well with some in the scene, particularly Active Dog's Ross Carpenter, who claimed Art had stolen its premise from him.

"I made the mistake of leaving my songbook at the practice space after writing a tune called 'Let's Go to Fuckin' Hawaii,' and, well, let's just say someone thought it was worth stealing," Carpenter said in 2010. "Art and I have come to an understanding recently about the song, but not many people realize that I wrote 'Hawaii.' It was going to be an Active Dog song."

For his part, Art later acknowledged that Carpenter did provide the song's inspiration—enough to be given a co-writing credit.

Art's proposed, and ultimately rejected, cover for the *Hawaii* EP. (Bev Davies)

Ross Carpenter did write a lot of "Hawaii." I added B sections. I saw it in a book, just the title, when I was blind drunk and took it. There is no argument at all.

Regardless of its origins, "Hawaii" provided both an ironic title and a visual element for the EP in keeping with the band's attitude, though Art's idea of a cover displaying a Bev Davies photo of him lying on a beach, naked and bound, was shot down. Driven by Rock's production, *Hawaii* solidified the Young Canadians' position at the vanguard of Vancouver punk when Quintessence released it in early 1980, in an initial pressing that also included leftover copies of the K-Tels single.

Rock recalled, "I'm sure the *Hawaii* sessions took place in the early evening after the commercial side of the studio closed, and we just set up and recorded. All I ever tried to do, and I think I did with them, was to incorporate the things I'd learned and at the same time try to emulate what was happening in England and New York. I was just trying to copy everybody. We captured the four songs in one go, and maybe spent another few days at the most fixing mistakes and mixing. I was really flying by the seat of my pants, but looking back, that EP always holds up for me, and I don't know why."

The fact that "Hawaii" became so popular bothers me because I've written a lot better songs. Not just that, but that EP sold about five thousand copies, and I never saw a cent of it.

Certainly, the dawning of the new decade held a lot of promise for many Vancouver bands. The Pointed Sticks became the first Canadian act signed to the powerhouse British indie label Stiff Records, while alliances strengthened in San Francisco through the Dead Kennedys, and in LA through Black Flag, leading D.O.A. to play an important role in establishing a North American punk touring circuit. Meanwhile, at home it seemed like the first wave of bands was finally gaining acceptance in the wider music industry. As John Armstrong said, "Everybody in that early independent scene owes a great deal to Les Wiseman and Tom Harrison and other people in the local press that actually supported us. The attitude was, like, 'We're going to shut this shit down now before it gets started.' There was an absolute stone wall. It wasn't until about two years later that all of these nightclub and band managers had an open meeting at a club downtown and wanted to get us in on the circuit, and hire us to go on the tours they would set up."

One of the forces driving that change was concert promoter Norman Perry, who, along with his brother-in-law at the time Riley O'Connor, launched Perryscope Concert Productions in 1977. Perry had gotten his feet wet in the concert promotion game by setting up events at his high school, before moving to

The Young Canadians with The Payola$, presented by Perryscope.

England and finding work on tours by major artists such as Pink Floyd. Returning to Canada, Perry joined up with powerful Montreal-based promoter Donald K. Donald and was put in charge of his first Vancouver show when Kiss played the Pacific Coliseum in 1977. It wasn't a sellout, and $8,000 of the gross had to pay the overtime for an unnecessarily large police presence. In the end, it was an important lesson for Perry about what the Vancouver market could bear, and at the start of 1978 he decided to take a different approach with Perryscope by enticing new-wave artists to add tour stops in Vancouver and other Western Canadian cities by playing venues they could reasonably expect to fill through affordable ticket prices. The company's Cheap Thrills concert series proved to be a big success, and Perryscope became the first promoter in Vancouver to present artists such as Patti Smith, Talking Heads, and Tom Petty & the Heartbreakers, all at the Commodore Ballroom.

For local bands, the side benefit of Perryscope's success was that they would often get tapped to be the opening act if a headliner was touring on their own. The Young Canadians got their first opportunity in March 1980, after receiving a call to accompany XTC on a string of dates. The British new-wave band was then at its commercial peak with the album *Drums and Wires* and the single "Making Plans for Nigel," which nearly scraped into the top 10 on the national Canadian radio chart. Perryscope set up six shows from Winnipeg to Victoria, with the Young Canadians opening nearly all of them. Overall, it was an enjoyable experience from Barry Taylor's perspective. "They were all really nice guys, we got along well, and the shows were great. We didn't go as far as Winnipeg with them; I think we went back to Calgary to play the infamous Calgarian, the dive punk-rock bar downtown."

A few weeks later, the Young Canadians got another chance to get out of town, this time opening seven shows for the Boomtown Rats. The Dublin-based band led by Bob Geldof—who had lived in Vancouver during the mid-1970s while serving as the *Georgia Straight*'s music editor—was also at that moment experiencing an unlikely commercial breakthrough with "I Don't Like Mondays," a song inspired by a school shooting in California the previous year. They were a bigger draw than XTC, and the Young Canadians found themselves playing theatres and arenas for the first time, while dealing with an entirely different breed of rock star. "Bob Geldof was cool, he was kind of quiet and kept to himself, but the rest of the guys in that band were fucking assholes," Taylor said. "They would leave us only ten minutes to set our gear up and were just generally standoffish, which was in complete contrast to XTC, who couldn't have been more friendly and accommodating. Thinking about it later, it seemed like it was a matter of confidence. XTC knew they were really good and weren't egotistical about it, whereas with the Boomtown Rats, I don't think they felt they could live up to the hype they were getting at that point."

As could have been predicted, the situation with the Boomtown Rats brought out Art's worst tendencies, and he got a modicum of payback at the April 3 show at Edmonton's Northlands Coliseum. "One of the habits we got into when we played those big venues was to explore them just as a way to kill time," Taylor explained. "So that night, I remember we all got up into the rafters somehow after we played our set. Art was pretty drunk by then and, well, when you gotta go, you gotta go. He started pissing on the stage as the Rats were playing, but we were so high up I don't think anybody noticed."

The experience of playing in arenas was so disheartening that later in the year they turned down a chance to be added to the bill when XTC returned as the opening act for the Police at the Pacific Coliseum. "Another reason we turned that down was because we didn't want to be associated with the Police," Taylor said. "I ended up going to the show just to see XTC and say hi, but I left when the Police came on. There was also talk that Perryscope wanted us to make our Toronto debut opening for Max Webster at Maple Leaf Gardens. I can't imagine how that would have gone, but we never made it to Toronto. The furthest east we got was Winnipeg."

It was much more satisfying for the Young Canadians to take opportunities to slip across the US border and play down through Washington, Oregon, and California, either tagging along with the Pointed Sticks or on their own after Bescott set up shows simply by calling venues. They were always welcome to stay at the San Francisco abode of the Dead Kennedys' Jello Biafra and Klaus Flouride, and in LA at the apartment shared by two Vancouver punk peers, D.O.A. and Avengers guitarist Brad Kent and drummer Bill Chobotar, better known as Zippy Pinhead. There, they also made connections with members of Black Flag, as well as with the Germs, just prior to their singer Darby Crash's suicide in December 1980.

Indeed, the border seemed irrelevant when it came to west-coast punk rock. Relationships were instead largely defined by someone's level of commitment to remain outside the commercial recording industry. Slowly but surely, though, bands found themselves on the major labels' radar, including the Payola$, who accepted an offer from A&M to record a four-song EP in 1980. All signs pointed toward Young Canadians manager Gerry Barad cutting a label deal as well, particularly after they had gone back to Little Mountain Sound with Bob Rock to record four new songs for their next Quintessence EP.

The evolution from the previous year's sessions, in terms of both songwriting and production, was clearly evident on "Data Redux," a hard-driving rocker that climaxed with Art's refrain "I fell in love with the enemy!" Its intensity was complemented by "Don't Bother Me," another of Art's instantly hummable put-downs, now given added sonic sugaring by Rock's increasing grasp of Little Mountain's capabilities.

The other two songs were Bescott's, "Just a Loser" and "This Is Your Life," with the latter ultimately chosen to be the EP's title track. It was a noble show of solidarity by the band, but by the time of *This Is Your Life*'s release in September 1980, cracks were starting to appear in the facade. In Taylor's view, although the trio was always committed to the band, their distinct personalities meant that their personal lives didn't overlap much beyond that. There were also signs that Bescott was struggling with his mental health. "When you combine that with alcohol, it can lead to some ugly scenes, and there were a couple of times when Art and I had to restrain him," Taylor said. "But throughout the life of that band, I would spend all of my time with my family when we weren't working, while Art would hang out with his White Rock buddies. I think it just reached a point where he was having more fun with them. Then again, I've been told that whenever something starts getting too big for him, he'll move on to doing something else. There were strong indications that we would make a full album at some point—the songs were definitely getting a lot more interesting—but we just couldn't keep it together."

One of the final Young Canadians shows, opening a new Vancouver venue, The Laundromat.

Things were still firing on all cylinders in the immediate wake of *This Is Your Life*'s release, when the Young Canadians played an all-Canadian bill at San Francisco's Mabuhay Gardens with D.O.A. and John Armstrong's new band the Modernettes. Their ragged, fiery set opened with Bescott's revealing "Mental Instability," before Art took the mic for "Beg, Borrow or Steal," a song that displayed the post-punk direction in which the band was clearly heading. Yet, within weeks the Young Canadians announced a multi-night farewell stand at Vancouver's Lotus Gardens Hotel, with a final bow on December 13.

By then, Taylor and Art had both made peace with putting the band to rest, but for Bescott the breakup marked a retreat to his adolescent Kitsilano neighbourhood and a decades-long battle with his demons. It came to a tragic end in 2005, when, mere weeks after a fire destroyed his mother's home, he died after being run over by a truck in a supermarket parking lot. As tributes poured in from the Vancouver music community, many were reminded of the Young Canadians' importance. Music critic Mike Usinger later wrote in the *Georgia Straight*: "As essential as its short-and-sweet catalogue might be, the band never made a perfect record during its short time together. If that sounds harsh, it's not meant to be. It's more of a reflection that, when the Young Canadians were great, they were fucking devastating."

> I was led to the belief that I had to leave because of our manager, Gerry Barad, who was straight out of Hollywood casting. Jim Bescott was an angel sent to me by I don't know who. I was the bitch who couldn't figure how to get along with a troubled genius and I regret it to this day. Narcissism was my disease and I am still hoping to cure myself of it.

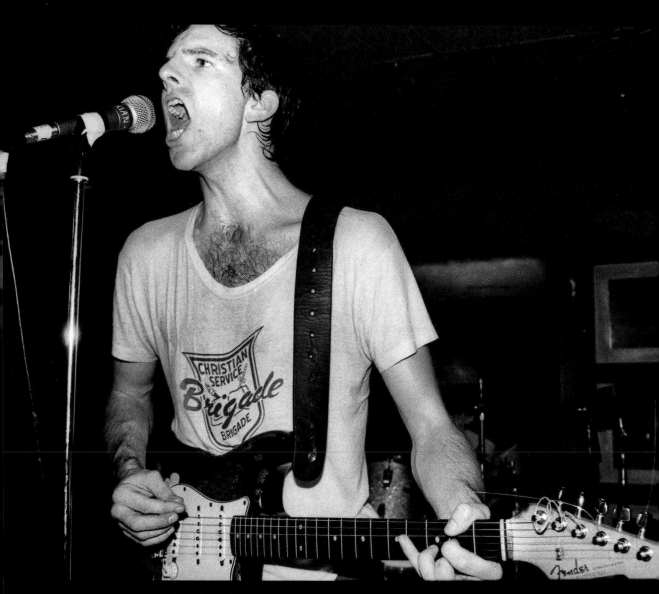

At the last Young Canadians show, The Lotus Gardens Hotel, December 13, 1980. (Bᴇᴠ Dᴀᴠɪᴇs)

SEISMIC SHIFTS

THE ORIGIN OF CANADA'S HEROIN LAWS can be traced back to the summer of 1907, when a contingent of Vancouver trade unionists and hooligans, working in cahoots with a similar group in San Francisco, organized themselves as the Asiatic Exclusion League. Their intent was to drive Chinese and Japanese immigrants from the city, and on the night of September 7, a mob of several thousand, inflamed by a flurry of racist speeches, invaded Vancouver's Chinatown and Japantown, causing widespread damage to businesses before police—by all accounts reluctantly—restored order.

Those whose livelihoods were affected rightly demanded reparations. Their appeal was passed on to the federal government, and within weeks, Minister of Labour William Lyon Mackenzie King arrived from Ottawa to assess the situation. Two opium manufacturers, working in an industry that up until then had operated with impunity, had made the largest claims—$600 each. While weighing that matter, King heard from members of the local Anti-Opium League, who spoke in desperate tones of how opium addiction was eroding their community. The plea worked; King could not morally justify spending taxpayer funds to prop up the opium businesses that sold their product not only to Asians, but to white men and women as well.

Upon his return to the capital, King filed a report stating: "This industry, I believe, has taken root and has developed in an insidious manner without the knowledge of the people of this country. Its baneful influences are too well known to require comment. The present would seem an opportune time for the government of Canada and the governments of the provinces to co-operate with the governments of Great Britain and China in a united effort to free the people from an evil so injurious to their progress and well-being."

Despite the rise of opiate addiction in urban areas potentially affecting North American trade with China—primary source of the poppies that yielded the raw ingredient—in 1908 King helped draft the Opium Act, outlawing the narcotic and its most potent powdered form, heroin, in Canada. The law's enactment came one year before the US spearheaded the International Opium Commission in Shanghai, regarded as the first concerted effort to regulate the use of non-medicinal narcotic substances. Recommendations by that commission were ratified in 1912 and adopted globally through their inclusion in the 1919 Treaty of Versailles. By then,

Canada had modified its Opium Act to also outlaw the production and sale of cocaine. Later, in 1923, it did the same for cannabis.

The Opium Act remained virtually unchanged until 1961, when Canada's Progressive Conservative government, under Prime Minister John Diefenbaker, updated it as the Narcotic Control Act in order to rein in the many varieties of synthetic opiates that had been created over the previous three decades. The new law—enacted at the urging of the United Nations—also took a harder line on marijuana, which until then accounted for only two per cent of all drug arrests per year in Canada. After 1961, that number steadily increased from low double digits to over five thousand marijuana-related arrests in 1970 alone. Heroin-related offences stayed at a low level by comparison, with a conviction for possession carrying a potential seven-year prison term. Someone caught with more than three grams of heroin could be charged with trafficking and faced a life sentence.

However, those threats did little to deter the suppliers and addicts who began significantly increasing in number throughout Vancouver's Downtown Eastside following the Second World War. The area was the city's oldest neighbourhood and the original heart of its downtown district, but as businesses gradually shifted westward to the entertainment strip on Granville Street, the Downtown Eastside's downward spiral accelerated. Its free fall was already under way during the 1930s, when scores of men looking for work found cheap accommodation in the many rooming houses there. Alcoholism flourished as a result, and by the mid-1960s the Downtown Eastside was primarily populated by older, single men—some still able to work in the fishing and forestry industries, but most now unemployed with no viable skills.

They became easy prey for heroin dealers working for the criminal factions that had infiltrated the Port of Vancouver, a process facilitated by lax union rules that allowed members to recommend friends, relatives, and associates for key positions as foremen, equipment operators, and truck drivers. In many cases, these ties led back to Hells Angels chapters and other local motorcycle clubs, who ran similar smuggling operations in the ports of Halifax and Montreal. With these connections, it became easy for untold amounts of heroin, cocaine, and the raw materials to produce them to enter Canada in the anonymous shipping containers coming from China or India. A 1994 report from the Ports Canada Police stated: "For many years, it was known that a number of longshoremen on the [Vancouver] port were affiliated with the Hells Angels. Numerous times, thefts of containers and their goods had been attributed to the Angels and their inside men. Unfortunately, a detailed list of these past incidents would take up too much room."

The report continued: "Angels are among the first to board arriving ships. They unload goods, place them for storage, load them onto trucks and prepare the necessary documents for shipping. They intimidate fellow workers, both on the docks and in the offices, with threats of violence and death, and have successfully imposed a forced code of silence on the port."

These efforts meant that by the 1970s, heroin could be easily procured in Vancouver and throughout the Lower Mainland by anyone interested in trying it. "There would be times when we would do whatever was available," Murphy Farrell recalled. "We'd snort coke or do acid and MDA. For us, it was experimenting. But even back in the early days, there were people around the scene who were into doing junk. They were not my friends, or our friends, but Art had this girlfriend who dabbled in it. I vividly remember him saying one day, 'I want to try some too,' and I said, 'Don't you fucking go down that road.' He still may have done it, but I never knew about it. When he moved to Vancouver, there were obviously a whole new set of influences, and once he started making a name for himself, different people started hanging on to him."

ooooo

Barry Taylor also sensed the increasing presence of the drug. "I didn't really notice any evidence of hard drugs starting to creep in until maybe a year and a bit after we'd been together. When you start touring and playing lots of shows, it starts to become a different world when you come home. People handle it differently; some just want to chill out and some want to go on a four-day bender. I noticed a few instances that Art was possibly into something, but it never interfered with the band. It wasn't until after the Young Canadians broke up that one day I was doing a session at this little studio called Andromeda Sound, and when it was over I decided to ride my bike over to this place nearby on Richards Street we called the Hacienda, where a lot of people from the scene were living. The door was open and I walked up the stairs, and when I came in, there were Art and Pinhead and bunch of other people lying around. Right then I said, 'Okay that's enough for me.' It had just devolved into debauchery."

It was always important to Art to maintain a social life detached from the Young Canadians. What made that easy was the fact that so many of his friends from White Rock were now fully immersed in their own creative pursuits, for which Art made himself available whenever possible. Another of these friends was Jim Cummins, who was a couple of years younger than Art and had been introduced to the Mount Lehman scene by one of its main LSD suppliers, Danny Clark. A gifted visual artist, Cummins occasionally drew flyers for Mt Lehman Grease Band gigs and, like others, made the move to Vancouver in 1977. Cummins at first wanted to be Vancouver punk's resident photographer, but he was soon swept up by the notion of forming his own band.

As Cummins said in a 1985 interview with CITR: "I was sharing a place with John Armstrong in the basement of the Manhattan [an apartment building on Thurlow Street], and after many a drunken evening we decided to form the ultimate punk band for the city, a band bent on destroying anything sacred, and ultimately even itself. We came up with the most vile name we could think of, the Braineaters, and started writing some songs. I'd only just gotten a guitar that summer and was learning how to play, so we got some other people involved, including Art Bergmann."

The Braineaters made their live debut in autumn 1979 and mere weeks later booked a session at Sabre Sound, where they cut five blistering songs short enough to fit onto a 7-inch single. As vocalist, Cummins was credited as Jim Cum, while Armstrong (on bass) was listed under his nom de punk, Buck Cherry. Guitarist Dave Gregg, on loan from D.O.A., was suitably credited as Dave By Proxy, and drummer Ian Tiles from the Pointed Sticks was listed simply as I.T. Art, who played keyboards in the group, appeared as Art Bormann. With the vinyl pressed, Cummins designed a silk-screened manila envelope to be reproduced as a sleeve, featuring a collage of Canadian $20 bills with pictures of various faces superimposed over Queen Elizabeth's image. It echoed the work the Sex Pistols' visual collaborator Jamie Reid and his use of *détournement*, the technique of manipulating familiar, often copyrighted imagery for satirical purposes. Cummins had his own sharp-edged style, though, which came to represent the Vancouver punk aesthetic more vividly than the short-lived original lineup of the Braineaters (later known as I, Braineater) ever did.

In Les Wiseman's assessment, "Jim Cummins was the conduit from the punk scene to the punk-friendly gay and discotheque venues. He was immediately recognized by the older generation of the Vancouver art scene—Alan Wood and Bill Featherston were fans from the first. He was also constantly marketing himself and thus was able to make a living from his art. It provided him a secure position in Vancouver, meaning he never made the move to New York, where he could have attained true international stardom."

For Art, being involved with the Braineaters was exactly the kind of situation he relished in a lot of ways, creating music with friends without any pressure to be the one in charge. As it became apparent a year later that the Young Canadians' days were numbered, finding that kind of situation again proved much more tempting than trying to forge ahead with a band whose members essentially had little in common. Others in the scene who shared Art's sentiments started finding each other as well, forming new alliances in order to play "just for the fuck of it," which led to certain groups being deemed "fuck bands." For most of these musicians, this new scene provided a welcome distraction from the intensity that was implicit at hardcore shows, and they were greatly encouraged by Bud Luxford, a brash young promoter whose intention was to inject some tongue-in-cheek show-business flair into the music. As Nick Jones, lead vocalist of the Pointed Sticks, explained, "When you live in a city that's six hundred miles away from the nearest other gig, after a while you can't keep playing your own original songs to the same crowd over and over again. So members of different bands would join together and form other little weird bands, mostly playing cover tunes or writing silly little songs, nothing really serious at all. I didn't have to be Nick Jones, lead singer of the Pointed Sticks. I could be Steve Roughhouser, drummer for Rude Norton, instead. Everyone got to take on different personas."

Although in some ways the Braineaters fit the profile of a fuck band, their stance remained rooted in punk dogma. The first true fuck band was indeed Rude Norton, which recorded a five-song 7-inch at Sabre Sound in autumn 1979. The tracks included revved-up versions of the Frankie Ford standard "Sea Cruise" and the themes to both *Gilligan's Island* and *Green Acres*. The last two, along with the Ramones-esque original "Tits on the Beach," would be added to the 2005 CD reissue of *Vancouver Complication*.

As the fuck-band movement continued to grow over the ensuing year, the Pointed Sticks were realizing their deal with Stiff Records wasn't panning out as they'd hoped, prompting bassist Tony Bardach to become open to new opportunities. The same could be said of drummer Zippy Pinhead/Bill Chobotar, who had moved back to Vancouver when his tenure with San Francisco's the Dils ended with their breakup in 1980, following the recording of the

Made in Canada EP with Bob Rock. A year later, the Dils' leaders, brothers Chip and Tony Kinman, would team up with Alejandro Escovedo of San Francisco punks the Nuns to form Rank and File, one of the first bands to establish the "cowpunk" genre, which introduced country-and-western elements. Meanwhile, Bill Scherk was still on the hunt for something substantial since the demise of Active Dog, and John Armstrong seemed to be an imminent free agent, as all signs were indicating that the Modernettes were on the outs.

> I didn't really hang out with those guys [in the Young Canadians]. We were just three mismatched personalities that played really well together but didn't hang out together. I wanted a band to be a band that I hung out with—like, if you don't show up with beer, or any other substance that would do as a substitute, then you're out of the band. That was my credo.

One of the first Los Popularos appearances in 1980, when they were still known as "Los Radicos Popularos".

Art, Armstrong, Scherk, Bardach, and Chobotar began getting together casually to jam and at first adopted the suitably tossed-off name the Popular Boys, which soon mutated into Los Radicos Popularos to stay consistent with the name of their home base, the Hacienda. The Mexican banditos motif stuck for a while, reinforced by noted Vancouver photographer Alex Waterhouse-Hayward, who, for a shoot to accompany the band's first appearance in Les Wiseman's *Vancouver* magazine column, adorned them in sombreros, along with antique bandoliers and Winchester rifles. As Chobotar stated in a 1983 CITR interview, "Things at that early stage were not very serious. We would play in people's living rooms with acoustic guitars, dressed up as Mexicans. We managed to pay our hydro bill that way."

Bill Scherk recalled: "The songs came out before there was a Los Popularos. Our very early material was built around 'Let's give Bill some backup to his humming. Let's help him get together something on tape, and then let's get that on a stage.'"

Within a month of the final Young Canadians shows, Los Popularos made their debut recording, appropriately titled "Hacienda," at Jim Cummins's home studio for the first *Bud Luxford Presents…* fuck-bands compilation album, released in January 1981. As the record's opening song, "Hacienda" clearly set a completely different tone with its Spanish-style acoustic guitar flourishes and the group harmony on the chorus of "Come and visit with your friends," sounding more foreboding than inviting.

"Jim Cummins had a little four-track studio in his house on Gore Avenue, and it was around Christmas time when everybody was really bored, so Bud went, 'Why don't we make an album of all these bands,'" Nick Jones recalled. "There were seven or eight bands already that could do something, and then three or four more just made themselves up on the spot."

Los Popularos, early 1981. L-R: John Armstrong (Buck Cherry), Bill Chobotar (Zippy Pinhead), Bill Scherk (Bill Shirt), Tony Bardach (seated), Art. (ALEX WATERHOUSE-HAYWARD)

Although "Hacienda" did capture the initial spirit of Los Popularos, in the weeks that followed the arrival of *Bud Luxford Presents...* in local shops, the band was ready to present itself as a serious undertaking at a handful of tentative live appearances where they premiered new, original material. Nobody who showed up had any idea of what the band would do, and in some ways neither did the members, though it was apparent that they wanted to move beyond the scorched-earth approach of their previous bands and attempt something more sophisticated.

"There were five pretty strong personalities in Los Popularos," Tom Harrison said. "Yes, they were all friends, but I got a sense right from the beginning that each of them harboured feelings that they were going to guide the creative direction. For fans of the Young Canadians and Art in particular, like me, it did seem like a curious decision for him to make, because you could see that the Young Canadians were on an upward trajectory before they split up. What they did was so intense, but Los Popularos wasn't intense at all. It was almost like an interruption to what Art was doing."

Nonetheless, the band's formal unveiling on February 24, 1981, was a major event for the scene with all press outlets in the city invited. It took place at a new all-ages venue called the Laundromat, a former dance studio on Richards Street that had opened the previous December with one of the Young Canadians' last gigs. A local cable television show was also on hand to record Los Popularos' debut for posterity. It was obvious that they'd put some thought into the overall presentation; each member wore a sharply tailored monochromatic suit, with the tall, lanky lead vocalist Bill Scherk doing his best to channel Bryan Ferry and Thin White Duke–era Bowie. At the same time, the guitar interplay between Art and Armstrong was something novel for both of them, though utterly natural given their history as teacher and student. With an emphasis on melody and dramatic lyrics, Los Popularos definitively demonstrated they were more than a fuck band. This was something with the potential to open a new chapter for the Vancouver scene, which now encompassed several distinct identities.

Manager Bruce Allen's dominance of the commercial rock world remained unquestioned, as his latest charges, Loverboy and Bryan Adams, increasingly became staples on US radio. Allen had taken a meeting with the Young Canadians following their *Georgia Straight* Battle of the Bands win, but both parties tacitly acknowledged any sort of partnership would have been a disaster. In Tom Harrison's view, "Bruce and Art are two strong-willed people, so I don't think they ever would have clicked in terms of a business relationship. The bottom line with Bruce is that he respects success, and sometimes it doesn't matter how good or bad the stuff is. I think if D.O.A.'s music was a little easier for people to take, Bruce might have considered working with them, but if Bruce had wanted Art to become, say, the next Bryan Adams, Art would have had to have made a lot of concessions, which, as most people who know him would agree, he never could have done."

It was left up to Bob Rock and Paul Hyde's Payola$ to take Vancouver punk mainstream with the release of their debut album *In a Place Like This* on A&M Records, while D.O.A. steadfastly held its position at the vanguard of the underground with the landmark album *Hardcore '81*, thirteen under-two-minute songs that some future punk scholars would credit for establishing the punk subgenre hardcore.

Meanwhile, the Quintessence Records label experiment was over. Despite their noble intentions to work with the Vancouver punk community, Ted Thomas and Gerry Barad never sold enough product to recoup the money they poured into each project, and eventually found themselves diverting funds from the retail operation to pay off debts. The pair was ultimately forced to concede defeat by shutting down the store and filing for bankruptcy. The lease was soon taken up by their employee Grant McDonagh, who aimed to learn from past mistakes by reopening under the name Zulu Records and, within a few years, making another attempt at operating a label as an extension of the store.

Roy Atkinson's crosstown shop Friends Records maintained relationships with D.O.A., the Subhumans, and a few others, helping to put out their product for the short-term on his Friends imprint, but most of the new Vancouver bands were on their own in finding financial backing. A new cluster of artists without explicit ties to the original Vancouver punk scene formed a collective called MoDaMu—short for "Modern Dance Music"—that pooled resources to fund projects and stage events. One of the collective's founders, Allen Moy, sang in the band Popular Front, which christened the MoDaMu record label with its debut single, "Doomsday Army," but the mandate held that everyone involved with MoDaMu had to work together for the benefit of all. Nonetheless, by 1982, one of the collective's bands from the suburb of Tsawwassen called 54-40 was showing the most potential on the strength of an EP and full-length album, prompting Moy and fellow musician Keith Porteous to become their full-time co-managers. Within a few years, they would launch 54-40 to national prominence upon securing a North American deal with Warner/Reprise Records.

Although the buzz surrounding Los Popularos continued to build into the spring of 1981, it wasn't translating to significant offers. After headlining two nights in early March at Gary Taylor's Rock Room, with 54-40 opening, and making a one-off jaunt across the border with D.O.A. to play at Evergreen State College in Olympia, Washington, on March 14, the band scrounged up enough money to book time at Ocean Sound in Kitsilano, a studio that had become a viable option for bands on low budgets when arrangements couldn't be made at Little Mountain Sound. Los Pops, as they were now commonly known, recorded two songs at Ocean Sound with producer Andy Graffiti, "Working Girls" and "Mystery to Myself," that were quickly pressed as a single and available by April.

As with the band's live show, anyone who may have been expecting some kind of magical amalgamation of the Young Canadians, the Modernettes, and the Pointed Sticks did not get it on the single. "Working Girls" was built around the familiar kick-and-snare drum opening of the Ronettes' "Be My Baby," and proceeded to establish a midtempo groove over which Scherk sang of his passion for the straitlaced women in Vancouver offices, with the others chiming in behind him on harmonies.

Los Popularos play Gary Taylor's Rock Room, with the fledgling 54-40 opening.

Art with *enfant terrible* drummer Bill Chobotar (Zippy Pinhead). (Bᴇᴠ Dᴀᴠɪᴇs)

"Mystery to Myself" offered something a little darker and more complex, but the idea still seemed to be placing Scherk's crooning abilities at the forefront, while Art and Armstrong picked up the slack with some interwoven, Keith Richards–style guitar parts. It all came off as strangely innocent and unconvincing, considering their individual pedigrees. Still, Los Popularos was now officially in the marketplace, with only forward progress to be made—if they could stay focused.

> We would play for pitchers of margaritas. What a cheap band we were. We were aggressively anti-social, but Bill was the opposite. Zippy Pinhead was this *enfant terrible*, just a fucking party machine. I remember one time rolling in broken glass at a Subhumans gig. That was fun. I think I was snorting amyl nitrite—that rush stuff kids do in the locker room. You go into blackout when you do that. That whole time's a fucking blur.

Los Popularos posters.

According to Les Wiseman, "I think it was in the first piece I did on Los Popularos that Art said they were all alcoholics and chain smokers who would have been hanging out together anyway, so why not start a band —a real band. I found that kind of telling." Wiseman added: "The early gigs I remember seeing weren't particularly well attended. They were in these strange, low-rent kinds of venues. I don't know if audiences really knew what to make of Bill Scherk as a lead singer."

In some respects, Los Popularos' inherent contradictions appeared to feed into the decadence they projected, which was far from a mere image. By the start of summer 1981, several of the members had moved into Scherk's apartment above a clothing store called, ironically, The Shirt Man, and were involved in relationships with prostitutes, another ironic twist on the theme of "Working Girls." There was also at least one non-musical tenant who people often came to visit.

"There was a guy who lived at The Shirt Man who passed himself off as their de facto manager, the guy who was really going to take them places," Wiseman said. "I would actually buy speed from him, but he was into a lot of other stuff. There was a pretty heavy atmosphere around that place."

Tom Harrison also recalls this darker turn. "Heroin was definitely a problem within the Vancouver punk scene by the start of the 1980s, mainly just because so much of it was coming in through the port," he said. "There was one guy in particular who was a self-styled filmmaker who thought that if he sold enough heroin, he'd have enough money to make this movie he had planned. Because of that, he became a pusher and a lot of people within the music scene became addicts as a result."

The heavy atmosphere surrounding the Hacienda eventually led to some far-reaching thinking about how Los Popularos might actually serve as a front for some of the illegal activities going on around them. If they could somehow fulfill their commercial potential through a modest investment, then who knew how much clean money they could ultimately rake in? After all, rock and roll wasn't brain surgery.

The plan got into motion with the purchase of a 1969 Oldsmobile Vista Cruiser—christened "Maria Vista Cruise"—to serve as the band's touring vehicle. Somehow, they managed to fit into it all five members, plus the gear and enough refreshments to keep everyone sated. "We did a lot of university shows, and we'd chum up with whoever we were staying with and talk them into giving us free beer from the campus bar," Chobotar recalled. "After the show, they'd fill up the old Popularos station wagon. We'd take the beer and party for three days or until the beer was all gone. That happened a lot with that band, even though we were always hanging by a wish and a prayer."

A lot of the bookings were made by Tony Bardach, who kept his contacts in a little black book. His method most often was to use pay phones and convince the operator to put the long-distance charges on a fake number in "Duck Ass Lake, Alberta" or some similar non-existent locale. For their first trip to Calgary, Los Pops shared the bill with a local punk band called the Presence, whose drummer Rob Hayter was a big Young Canadians fan. "I was barely eighteen years old in 1980 when I saw the Young Canadians open for XTC in Calgary," Hayter said. "I had seen a lot of big touring rock bands by then, but the Young Canadians grabbed my attention, not only because of their 'underground' status, but mostly because of Art. His stance, performance, passion, and playing style were unlike anything I had seen live. Physically, they didn't fit the giant stage, but Art's enormous and melodic songs and the incredible energy of the band impressively filled the void. Someone I knew had a copy of the *Hawaii* EP, and we listened to it quite a bit. Barry Taylor's 'take no prisoners' drumming style was an influence on me. A few weeks after the XTC show, the Young Canadians played the Calgarian, a dive hotel bar downtown that was the epicentre of Calgary's thriving underground punk and indie scene. Watching the band up close was equally enjoyable; Art, Jim, and Barry played every song as if their lives depended on it."

By the following year, Hayter was part of the Presence along with guitarist Brad "Spaz" Paffe, bassist Grant Sim, and vocalist Keith "K.G." Higgins, already known around town as a poet and performance artist. After releasing a five-song 7-inch called *Meeting the Demands of Society Is No Excuse*, they started venturing to the coast, where their connection with Los Popularos proved helpful. "The Presence travelled to Vancouver for a couple of gigs on our own at the Railway and the Smilin' Buddha, and played a gig in Seattle," Hayter said. "In Vancouver, we stayed at the Hacienda, crashing on the floor in this famous band house with a seemingly 24/7 party going on. Art lived upstairs in a room somewhere, and it was a lot of fun to mingle with the cream of the Vancouver indie scene. Our bands shared a mutual respect, a love of drinking and hardcore partying, musical mayhem, laughter, and dreams of greatness. Zippy Pinhead and I were certainly kindred spirits. The two bands differed greatly in musical style—Los Pops were graceful, elegant, smooth, and easy to consume, while the Presence was much more intense, frenetic, loud, funky, and downright strange at times. It was most noticeable in Bill Shirt's velvety vocals versus K.G.'s snarling urban angst. But opposites attract, right? Someone suggested we should tour together, and the stage was set."

For Los Popularos, and Art in particular, one of the main attractions of a tour was the prospect of finally making it to Toronto and seeing how much their reputation was worth, now that every major record label had established branch offices there. On Canada Day 1982, Los Pops joined the bill with D.O.A. for a show in Stanley Park dubbed "Rock the Boat," its purpose being to protest the growing threat of global nuclear war, stoked by the Thatcher regime's recent purchase of the US Trident submarine-launched missile system. Following that, the band made its final preparations for the trek east, adding a U-Haul box to the roof of the Vista

Cruiser for extra storage. After meeting up with the Presence, travelling with their gear in Hayter's 1968 Chrysler Newport, they set out for the first gig in Regina. "We played at the university," Hayter said, "a big room with a Prairie crowd of 'new wavers'—girls with spiky haircuts pogo-ing and guys with moustaches and mullets in punk rock T-shirts. I was surprised to be signing a few copies of our EP, my first taste of living the rock and roll dream. While there, we all crashed a gallery opening when we heard there was free food and booze. I remember Art leaning out the car window, shouting at some local girls, 'Does daddy know you took the combine to town?'"

Chobotar recalled a similar culture shock. "I remember we stopped at some dingy little roadhouse in Buttfuck, Saskatchewan, for beer, and three rednecks with John Deere hats stopped talking as soon as we walked in. I was still wearing a gold lamé shirt from the night before, and we were all wearing makeup and eyeliner. We looked like a low-budget Depeche Mode or something, and these rednecks were just staring at us. These guys couldn't believe what they were seeing, but then they realized that we were just as drunk and hungover as they were. Then it was okay and we got our beer with no extra trouble. We could hear them laughing as we left with a couple of two-fours."

The next dates were an extended run in Winnipeg at Wellington's, the basement bar in the St. Charles Hotel, where both bands had been assured accommodation. "We arrived in the very early morning, pre-dawn," Hayter said. "We were banging on the front door and ringing the bell until a little old lady appeared in her dressing gown. She was terrified at the sight of us, especially Art, Zippy, and Bill Shirt, all tall, blond guys in black leather. She screamed at us in broken English, 'No, no, I call police,' and a couple of Winnipeg's finest arrived shortly thereafter. We explained to the cops that we were the bands, booked to play for a few nights, and we wanted to check into our rooms. The cops went inside and spoke to the woman, Maria, then told us she was not going to let us into the hotel at night, and we would have to find somewhere else to go. Someone knew a guy in town named Brad Roberts, who would go on to form Crash Test Dummies, and he allowed us to stay in his basement. We returned to the hotel the next day, and the rest of the week went smoothly."

After the all-night parties that followed each performance, the musicians subsisted mainly on doughnuts given to them by a generous female Tim Hortons employee down the street, whom the Presence's Grant Sim had befriended. Hayter added: "We would give some of them to Maria and her husband, Harry. One day, when we saw the tattoo on Harry's arm, we realized they were Holocaust survivors. Maria cried at our kindness in giving her our spare doughnuts, and we left Winnipeg on good terms."

From there, it was the twenty-four-hour drive to southern Ontario, and by the time they arrived in London for the next gig, road fever had firmly set in. During a breakfast stop, Art ordered pancakes "smothered in a Middle East peace settlement," much to the waitress's dismay. However, the show before a predominantly university-educated crowd went well, and the bands spent some time with New York City post-punks Certain General, whose drummer, Marcy Saddy, had previously played with Toronto's the 'B' Girls. It all seemed to bode well for their Toronto debut, although the best-laid plans, as they so often do, ultimately went awry.

"I don't remember where we played in Toronto—it was a gay bar full of art-school types," Hayter said. "I do remember partying later in a huge, old house somewhere, and on the way we were stopped by the cops. My car was searched for no good reason I could see except for the Alberta plates. All of us crashed in someone's fifth-floor apartment. The building owner was not happy about it and arrived to evict us with some thug he brought along. The thug shoved Art, who was barely awake. Art screamed, 'Touch me again and I will die on you, you fuck!' and the guy backed right off."

In Chobotar's view, "We were a lot more notorious with Buck Cherry in the band. We were like Vikings—raping and pillaging across the Prairies to Toronto. It was like one gigantic roller coaster that went on forever. So much alcohol and fun, with a smattering of music thrown in for good measure. The girls thought we were Canada's answer to Duran Duran, and they seemed to like us. Who were we to argue? We'd set out to be huge sluts, and we totally achieved that."

Well, not totally, at least from Art's perspective. With the Presence heading back to Calgary—playing at 7th St. Entry in Minneapolis with friends Hüsker Dü en route—Art's plan was to stay in Toronto and try to build a new network of connections for Los Popularos. For the others, that meant the party was over for all intents and purposes, as serious work now needed to be done in an environment none of them were familiar with. Although he could sense progress starting to be made after a couple weeks of hustling, the biggest score being a gig at Larry's Hideaway, Toronto's leading underground music club at the time, Art ultimately caved in to demands to go back to Vancouver.

> When we got to Toronto, we parked at Sherbourne and Wellesley and we drew straws every night to see who would stay in the car and watch our meagre possessions while the rest of us tried to find places to sleep. After two weeks, we had girlfriends, places to stay, and people coming to hear us. For some reason, we left. What a dumb idea.

"Rematch of the Century" poster. (COURTESY ROB HAYTER)

With Bardach hastily arranging gigs to pay their way back, they managed to purchase a 1975 Chevy Bel Air station wagon to replace the Vista Cruiser, which could carry them no further. Los Pops reunited with the Presence in Saskatoon, where they played together at the University of Saskatchewan, before the two bands had one final blowout in Calgary, billed as "The Rematch of the Century." The aftermath was more than a little bittersweet, particularly because none of the financial windfall they had all envisioned came to fruition. As he had done in the past, Art was willing to put music temporarily on hold in order to refill his depleted bank account, and informed the band he was going to stay in Calgary when Hayter told him he could find the two of them immediate, well-paid employment.

"I had a good friend, Rob Brink, who had a career working on seismic crews that did geological testing for big construction projects and oil companies. Rob arranged for Art and I to apply for jobs at Western Geophysical, working as 'jug hounds' on his crew. We applied and were duly hired, and before we knew it, we found ourselves in a camp at Mile 173 on the Alaska Highway in northern BC. It was completely surreal. Art likened it to working on a prison chain gang."

The pair had to quickly adapt to being awakened each morning at 6 a.m. and working with grizzled veterans whose jobs were simply described as "slashers" and "blasters." After several weeks under those harsh conditions, Art and Hayter begged the camp medic to take them in his ambulance to the nearest town with a liquor store, 150 kilometres away, in order to stock up on beer and Scotch.

"That changed the mood of the place," Hayter said. "We had gone on this adventure seeking solvency and sobriety. Well, the solvency part worked. But at nineteen, I was drinking like a sailor on shore leave. Hungover, the job became more bizarre. We were flying to the line in an ancient helicopter with a bent door, driving enormous track vehicles, listening to huge explosions, talking on radios, wiping our asses with moss, and eating enormous lunches with our colleagues in the freezing wilderness.

"Eventually one day, after some months, tired and jaded, Art decided he wanted to go home. Easily led, I agreed and we hatched a plan to escape. Our friendly ambulance driver gave us a ride to Fort St. John, three hours away, where we got on a flight to Edmonton, then to Calgary. How we paid for the tickets I have no idea—neither of us had credit cards. I just remember sitting in the Edmonton airport bar, still in our seismic gear, unshaven and stinky. We were drinking paralyzers, mouths agape, ogling the first women we'd seen in months. It was the end of a great adventure, truly our Fear and Loathing in the Great White North."

Once back in Vancouver, Art was forced to confront the individual who had been funding Los Popularos and try to explain why he wouldn't be seeing any return on his investment anytime soon. The dealer responded by pulling out a gun and making threats, leaving Art with no choice other than to calmly describe the realities of the music industry and why, especially in Canada, it was much less lucrative than everyone thought. Somehow, he made a convincing argument—no small feat, evidently, considering the dealer would receive a life sentence for murder a few years later.

With that matter thankfully settled, Art retained a sizable portion of his seismic earnings for the band, and Los Populoaros forged ahead into the final months of 1982 playing locally, but with a goal of making a new recording. In Art's absence, John Armstrong had decided that the Los Pops lifestyle he'd experienced on tour was not something he wanted to go through again, and he set about reconstituting the Modernettes. Los Pops, in turn, enlisted another old White Rock friend, Gord Nicholl, whose keyboards added a further dimension to the sound. Nicholl's addition also marked a more concerted effort to improve the overall quality of their next release, and they put in significant pre-production work on several songs at Ross Carpenter's home studio.

By late October, the band was set up at Ocean Sound, recording four original songs that would comprise an EP entitled *Born Free*. The results were indeed a vast improvement on the single from the previous year, with Art taking a more prominent role in Armstrong's absence. However, the opening track "Get Out of Your House" laid bare the predicament the band was in. As a galloping, guitar-driven rocker, it seemed to follow a Payola$-style template of utilizing a radio-friendly arrangement and production values while retaining just enough rough edges to avoid any accusation of selling out. It was a tightrope walk, to be sure, the same one that many other bands faced while navigating the post-punk landscape. Yet, Art's roots in '60s pop remained a significant touchstone on the jangly "Can't Come Back," a subtle nod to new-wave sensibilities, but sounding more in step with the nascent Paisley Underground movement emerging in southern California. That approach carried through on the more upbeat "Don't Say It," which watered down any traces of punk attitude altogether in favour of creating the sort of sexual tension expressed by the likes of Elvis Costello and Squeeze. Los Pops saved the most fury for "Out on the Frontier," a brooding track inspired by Art's seismic work, as evidenced by lines such as "I've come to lend a hand to aid this wretched land," and "The songs that gave me joy are fading in the noise." It concluded the EP on a suitably enigmatic note; Los Popularos now had a product that demonstrated their full dynamic range, but whether they could be classified as punk, new wave, or mainstream rock was still an open question.

To complicate matters further, *Born Free* was released in November 1982 in two distinct pressings, one on the band's own GP Productions label, with cover photographs of the members taken by Magdalena DiGregorio at a farm in Langley, and the other on the Toronto-based Sensible Records label, which featured entirely different artwork highlighted by a stark black-and-white image of a female model on the cover. The short-lived label was launched by Andrew Cash and Charlie Angus, idealistic founders of L'Etranger, who saw themselves as kindred spirits with Los Popularos and were among the few eager to make a connection during Los Pops' brief stay in Toronto.

The dual pressings underscored the lack of organization that continued to reveal itself as Los Popularos' Achilles heel. While *Born Free* became a favourite of campus radio programmers across Canada, a lack of distribution and commercial-radio promotion meant it would soon merely become the stuff of legend, available only to those tuned in to the proper channels. Art was directly hit with that harsh reality when Los Pops played with D.O.A. and I, Braineater at UBC on March 19, 1983, and a drunk audience member remained in his face during the entire set, screaming at him to play "Hawaii." The band soldiered on until the end of 1983, when any trace of fun had gone out of what had originally been a project based on friendship and collaboration. If Art was to continue making music, it would have to be on his own terms.

Early 1983 gig, with Gord Nicholl on keyboards in place of John Armstrong.

Like all great bands, we were pretty awful sometimes. In the end, we broke up because we couldn't record anymore. But it all really went to shit because I had all these songs that didn't suit the way Bill sang. It had to come across with more aggression.

LEGITIMATE BUSINESS

In 1982, THE BAND SCISSORS released its self-titled independent debut EP, putting itself in the running to be the next breakout Vancouver new-wave act. The odds were long, but group founder and lead singer/guitarist Billy Barker was determined to make something happen. He'd been in several bands dating back to the pre-punk days, but none of them had offered what the kids wanted to hear. As a result, when it was clear that tastes were broadening in the aftermath of punk's initial explosion, Barker sensed an opening for his brand of rough-edged, pop-infused rock and roll.

He called Ray Fulber, who had played bass in Nytro, one of those former projects of Barker's that had quickly fizzled out, and the pair started laying the groundwork for a new band that could get away with wearing leather jackets without having their songs pay lip service to punk's nasty politics. With the addition of keyboardist Jan Henriksen and drummer John Cody they became Scissors—not as dangerous as knives, but still a sharp object. The band was welcomed into the Vancouver punk community upon its unveiling at the start of 1981, making its first high-profile appearance at a "Rock Against Reagan" show in March at the Teamsters Hall, headlined by the Subhumans. About a year later, Scissors shared the stage with Los Popularos for the "Youth Explosion #1" show at the West End Community Centre, on a bill that also included the bands French Letters, featuring future 54-40 drummer Matt Johnson, and the Enigmas, whose drummer, Randy Bowman, had played with Barker and Fulber in Nytro.

But it was Los Popularos that had the biggest reputation at that point, and Fulber, for one, had been around the scene long enough to recognize that it stemmed directly from Art's songwriting. The pair forged a personal connection mainly on the basis of a shared understanding that punk meant something deeper than just *Never Mind the Bollocks* or having the right hairstyle. Yet, for the remainder of 1982, it seemed Los Popularos and Scissors were facing similar identity crises that could no longer be ignored in the recording studio. Fulber had built his own facility in East Vancouver, Profile, where Scissors cut the six tracks for their EP. The songs were all high-energy, springing from Barker's overactive impulses, as displayed on numbers like "Wrecked My Car," his bold-faced confession about his questionable driving skills.

The Scissors EP came out in November 1982, with the label bearing the band's own Zuma Records imprint, just as copies of Los Popularos' *Born Free* began circulating. Scissors would similarly be relegated to obscurity due to a lack of distribution and promotion, and by the following year Fulber could see no point in continuing to follow Barker's whims.

Meanwhile, as the dreaded Orwellian year 1984 dawned, Art was fully putting Los Popularos behind him. He had been writing songs drawn from the rubble of the previous three years, and was jamming with a new rogue's gallery of musicians, mostly from a band called Psychic Healers. The group included drummer Taylor Nelson Little, keyboardist Fred Hamilton, and guitarist Ted Rich, the last a volatile specimen who would come to discover that the source of his angst was largely the dark secret that he was, incredibly, Eric Clapton's half-brother. Rich's father was Montreal-born Edward Fryer, who, while serving in the Canadian army and stationed in England during the Second World War, impregnated sixteen-year-old Patricia Clapton during a brief tryst. To hide her shame, she consigned her baby to be raised in a traditional household by her mother and stepfather, and never revealed the truth to her child as Fryer did his duty in Europe and eventually continued to spread his seed back home in Canada.

As Art's vision for his latest band coalesced around one of his new songs, "Poisoned," he invited back figures from the past to participate in loosely scheduled demo recording sessions between February and May 1984, at engineer Cec English's eight-track studio, Civilian. Back on the scene were Pete Draper, Barry Taylor, and Gord Nicholl, with Bill Scherk contributing a few backup vocals to a couple of songs he, Art, and Nicholl had co-written. Being free of the constraints of Los Popularos was immediately evident; Art was back to spitting out his lyrics on all the material, though now the words stung with a fresh sense of musicality that fully incorporated his pop instincts. The timing seemed absolutely right, as artists like David Bowie and Elvis Costello had embraced a radio-friendly aesthetic, while the power of music videos provided countless other examples of artists formerly on the fringes now gaining new audiences simply by writing something catchy and presenting it in a visually compelling manner. Although the Young Canadians had appeared live on John Tanner and J.B. Shayne's pioneering cable-access music-video program *Nite Dreems* (along with its sister show, *Soundproof*), Art made his first attempt at a "proper" music video with the song "Emotion," teaming up with Stokely Seip, one of the earliest video directors in Canada, who had also shot clips for I, Braineater and Toronto avant-garde legend Nash the Slash. Although Art came across forcefully on film, the video's lasting value turned out to be simply capturing the short-lived post–Los Popularos band Art had pulled together.

Interview with *Discorder*, July 1984:
I don't know, I just want to get back to playing live and then do some recording in a 24-track, then we'll see what happens. It's tough to get back to being the focus of a band, singing and so on. It's a lot easier just staying in the back playing guitar and doing backups. But yeah, we'll see what happens.

Art remained adamant about maintaining a band dynamic, and "Poisoned" seemed as appropriate a name as any given Art's view of what the music industry did to people. The ten songs recorded throughout the spring were manufactured in a limited run of cassettes simply bearing the name "Poisoned," by which time Art was ready to get back into the clubs with a lineup consisting of Rich, Hamilton, Little, and bassist Murray Andrishak, an acquaintance from Calgary now in Vancouver.

"I was a Young Canadians fan, but I didn't meet Art until he was in Los Popularos," Andrishak said. "They played Calgary quite often, and Art was always a lot of fun to be around. There wasn't much of a scene there then, so for all of us who were in struggling bands, when Los Popularos came to town, they were like real rock stars."

Andrishak moved to Vancouver in 1983, and one day the following year encountered Art while riding his bike on Commercial Drive. "He told me about the Poisoned cassette he was putting out, and that he was looking for people to start a band with. He asked if I'd like to try out, and I said sure. I wasn't doing anything at the time, so I thought it would at least be good for kicks."

Andrishak was admittedly intimidated at the prospect of playing with Art, but he held it in check because of the band's overall enthusiasm and the initial response the cassette received. "There was definitely a buzz about it, and it seemed like we could do no wrong at first," he said. "Ted was a hell of a guitar player and he added a lot to the band. When he was there, all of the focus wasn't squarely on Art. But unfortunately, Ted was an excitable guy and there ended up being a lot of friction between he and Art when Ted would want us to play some of his songs."

With Rich gone and Hamilton soon to follow, the Poisoned lineup eventually stabilized with the addition of keyboardist Tom Upex—husband of Dishrags drummer Carmen "Scout" Michaud—and backup vocalist Virginia McKendry, another former Calgarian who had played in a string of country and punk bands since the late '70s. "Once those two were in the band, it became really diverse and interesting," Andrishak said. "That first six months was exciting in general. We got steady work pretty quickly and people were coming out to see us, I think mainly based on Art's reputation. I guess we looked the part, and it might have been a case of 'fake it until you make it.' But playing those songs made me realize what an amazing melodic sensibility Art had. I actually never listened to much punk rock, so I got a lot of enjoyment out of trying to make Art's songs sound as best as they could. Music was changing at that time, and I think we were well suited to be a part of that."

They demonstrated it when Perryscope Productions offered Poisoned the opening slot for the Psychedelic Furs at the Orpheum Theatre on August 11, 1984. As always with Art, what they weren't suited for was taking care of the business side of the band. Like most in the scene, Ray Fulber was aware of the buzz surrounding Poisoned, and when he noted how Art was struggling to take advantage of it, he saw an opportunity to offer some help. "I was working with a band called the Actionauts," Fulber recalled. "But they were having so many fights in the studio that I could see things weren't going anywhere, and that's when I started talking to Art. Scissors had done some gigs opening for the Young Canadians at high schools, and then later we did some bigger shows with Los Popularos, and that's how I met him. But during that period in '84, Art was actually living with some of the Actionauts at this place they had on Broadway. I was hanging around there a lot, so I said to Art, 'Look, I'm tired of fucking around with these guys. I've got all this time available at my studio before I sell it, so let's do an EP.'"

Art and Fulber shared many traits when it came to doing whatever was necessary to make music happen. Fulber was flush with cash at that moment from selling his stake in Profile, a deal that also allowed him a good chunk of time to keep recording there. This money was in addition to what Fulber made from his side business importing marijuana from Mexico. Soon, he and Art would also be doing heroin regularly together. Despite this, the pair remained focused on the task of making Poisoned the band that would finally get Art the recognition he deserved. They focused on recording six songs, three that had already appeared on the cassette—"It Won't Last," "Emotion," and "Yellow Pages"—and three new songs, "Pretty Beat" (co-written with Ted Rich), "Yea, I Guess," and "Guns and Heroin," the last a thinly veiled account of the Los Populares story and the deal that was made to bankroll the band: "Where did the money come from / Two weeks out of prison / Fifty dollars for a gun / Turned into fifty thousand / We met two mutual friends / She's a hooker I'm a musician / He wants legitimate business / God if he only knew it's the same as / Guns and heroin."

> Interview with *Western Front*, Bellingham, Washington, November 9, 1984: Now it's come back to being outrageous is to be normal. You just play as best you can. You don't need props, just be yourself. And writing songs is easy. You start with a conversation you heard the night before—if you can remember it. You pick up on the crazy things people say. There might be a theme or idea and then you have to flesh it out. It's like bullshitting on an exam. My style has always been the same, but I suppose I've gotten better. You try to get a fine edge in what you're trying to say. Every song has its own message.

Fulber was close with Bob Rock, and the producer—still a big fan of Art's—eagerly agreed to mix the tapes at Little Mountain Sound over the Christmas break on the studio's brand-new SSL board. "Bob Rock used to mix as loud as a concert at Little Mountain," Fulber said. "You could actually get a stomach ache sometimes when you went in there. Bob mixed louder than anyone I have ever heard. It was like being in the Commodore [Ballroom] but even louder. People had no idea, and that's how he was making those albums. He was like a live soundman—he would do it on the fly, going right onto the two-track tape. That's why bands like Aerosmith and Mötley Crüe liked working with him later on, because it was an approximation of their live show. I know there's more to it than that—Bob has great production skills—but when we'd walk into a control room with Bob mixing, it was a rush. You didn't need dope, it was a huge sound rush, and that always excited me."

When Rock was done, Fulber took the mixes to Los Angeles for mastering, while photographer Alex Waterhouse-Hayward staged a shoot for the EP's cover with an intent to echo the four dramatic, shadowed head shots of *With the Beatles* (Virginia McKendry had left the band by then). There was the additional element of a music video, which felt mandatory since the launch of MuchMusic in August 1984, a watershed moment that overnight connected all of Canada's disparate independent scenes, largely through the channel's need to fulfill Canadian-content broadcasting quotas. Fulber was able to pool the resources to make a video for the raucous track "Yea, I Guess," showing Poisoned playing in a surreal cabaret setting to an audience of outlandish characters. Dressed in then fashionable new-wave garb, with his blond locks cascading across his forehead Jerry Lee Lewis–style, Art gave an unhinged lip-synched performance that burned through the television screen.

Poisoned gig, 1985. The photo was taken from the cover of their EP.

Once again, the EP bore only the name "Poisoned," and with a run of copies pressed with Fulber's East-Ray imprint on the label, Ray organized a launch party at a large space that 54-40's management team ran as an off-licence, after-hours venue. He invited his lawyer, Susann Richter, to come out that night, at which point their relationship transitioned from professional to personal. Richter was a familiar presence in the Poisoned circle from then on.

All signs were pointing toward the band making an impact in 1985, the year that would be remembered for the music industry throwing its full resources behind Bob Geldof's crusade to ameliorate the African famine crisis. The Vancouver underground community did its small part by staging a benefit show for OXFAM at UBC's SUB Ballroom on February 23. Poisoned headlined a bill that also included the cream of the punk scene's next wave of bands: the explosive, prog-rock-informed NoMeansNo from Victoria, Family Plot and their two-bass/no-guitar lineup, the MoDaMu band Animal Slaves, and Shanghai Dog, which had recently enlisted Barry Taylor on drums. Aside from raising awareness for the cause, the show underscored the more experimental direction the original Vancouver sound had taken. In fact, an entirely separate scene was coalescing around the synthesizer-heavy band Images in Vogue, one of whose members, Kevin Crompton (a.k.a. cEvin Key), would go on to form the more aggressive and theatrical Skinny Puppy, the band that proved to be the catalyst for both the industrial music movement in North America and the creation of Nettwerk Records, whose co-founder Terry McBride would come to challenge Bruce Allen's position as Vancouver's most influential music industry figure.

Art and Fulber kept pushing to find a place for Poisoned within that milieu, but found themselves still mainly confined to playing the familiar northwest circuit. Nonetheless, they took every opportunity that presented itself. On September 26, 1985, the band was booked to play Hillside Secondary School in West Vancouver, an event organized by student John Ruskin. Ruskin had become a fan of Art's after noticing his school received a thank-you in the liner notes of the Young Canadians' *This Is Your Life* EP, for hosting one of their gigs. As a member of the student council, he was able to offer Poisoned $1,400 to play the school's first scheduled student dance of the year, and when the day arrived, Ruskin asked his friend Glen Winter to get his hands on a video camera and film Ruskin interviewing Art for the school's archives. It was the first interview Ruskin ever conducted in what would become a long and infamous career as his alter ego, Nardwuar the Human Serviette.

Everyone involved with Poisoned was conscious of playing too much in Vancouver, and by the end of the year Fulber threw financial caution to the wind by setting up a cross-Canada tour on his own and making sure Art and the band had sufficient gear to pull it off. For Murray Andrishak, that first Poisoned tour in the late winter and early spring of 1986 turned out to be a test of both his stamina and his loyalty. As he recalled, "We flew from Vancouver to Toronto, where we played the Horseshoe Tavern and Lee's Palace. Then we went to Montreal, where we did a gig at Concordia University and also a show at Les Foufounes Électriques. After that, I remember driving to Ottawa through an ice storm to play a club there. What stands out about that was we shared the bill with Handsome Ned, the country singer from Toronto. It was, sadly, pretty obvious to me that he was a heroin addict, and I think he ended up tagging along with us because he knew our reputation, and there would be drugs to be had if he hung around. He ended up actually playing acoustic guitar with us that night, and I really liked him. He was a very personable guy, and I was shocked when I found out later that he'd died from an overdose not long after that."

Andrishak, who was living a clean life and didn't even smoke cigarettes, was already well acquainted with the toll heroin was taking on the scene back in Vancouver. What he saw while on tour just confirmed his fears about getting too deep into that world. So, when keyboardist Tom Upex announced he was going to leave the band at the end of the tour, Andrishak saw his chance to get out as well. "Tom was probably my best friend out of everyone in the band, so I thought, if he's leaving, I'm not going to stick around. I had a job and was in a long-term relationship, and actually found the whole thing about being on tour really boring. I just wasn't into that party lifestyle, and in fact, I didn't play music again after that."

As Poisoned's manager, Ray Fulber was painfully aware of the growing rift in the band and was prepared to take the necessary steps to keep things moving forward. Andrishak had sensed this from the moment Fulber became part of the equation two years earlier. "Ray had deep pockets, and that was a godsend to Art, because he didn't have any money," Andrishak said. "When Ray came along, it became more of a business, but at the same time the hard-drug use wasn't as hidden anymore, and that was a big turnoff for me. I also didn't have a lot of self-confidence as a player, so when Ray took charge, it seemed the writing was on the wall for me. I was either going to be forced out or asked to leave and Ray was going to take over on bass. It was going to happen eventually, and I remember telling people at the time, 'Just watch, they're going to go through the charade of auditioning other bass players, but in the end they're going to go with Ray,' because he was paying for everything and made all the final decisions. And that's exactly what happened. But I don't harbour any bad feelings about it. I've always admired Art, and we stayed on good terms after that."

For Fulber, taking a more direct role in the band seemed necessary by that point to keep Art's creative juices flowing., "I met the band in Calgary for the last gig they did on their

In full throat with Poisoned (Bᴇᴠ Dᴀᴠɪᴇs)

way back," he said. "While we were partying in my hotel suite with a bathtub full of beer, some of Art's old fans were berating me for taking the 'punk rock' out of him. It pissed me off and I started throwing beers against the far wall and said, 'Is this what you mean by punk rock?' I had to pay $500 in damages for that."

As Poisoned regrouped with Fulber on bass and Gord Nicholl once again coaxed back into the fold to play keyboards, Ray rented the top floor of a building at 322 Water Street in Vancouver's Gastown neighbourhood, soundproofing it with a dumpster load of carpet samples from End of the Roll, and turning it into a rehearsal space not just for Poisoned, but for other bands that could pay to use it. Those funds, along with the new home base, allowed Art to work on new material, and by autumn 1986, Ray determined the time had come to go after a major-label record deal.

> There was never any plan toward securing a record deal. I thought it was a
> fun game to play. That's it, that's all, that's the whole of the law.

In October, Fulber approached Bob Rock and Paul Hyde to help make a four-song demo tape for Fulber to shop. Hyde agreed to produce the sessions at Ray's old studio, Profile, while Rock agreed to mix the tracks at Little Mountain. It was a savvy move on Fulber's part, given the Payola$ were then at their commercial peak, coming off the Juno Award–winning hit "Eyes of a Stranger" and their participation in creating Canada's official African famine benefit single, "Tears Are Not Enough." In fact, the Payola$' label, A&M, was so bullish on their potential to break on mainstream American radio that it urged Rock and Hyde to work with Victoria BC–born songwriter and producer David Foster, whose knack for composing treacly ballads for artists such as Chicago, Kenny Loggins, and Kenny Rogers was making him an untold fortune.

That plan would ultimately backfire on the Payola$, but having Rock and Hyde's names attached to Poisoned still seemed a surefire bet to gain record company interest. They focused on recording four of Art's new songs: "To Tell the Truth," "Blackhearts," "My Empty House," and "Runaway Train," all pleas from desperate individuals, conveyed by Art with the appropriate amount of bile and bitterness. Art's performances stood in contrast with Hyde's standard mid-'80s, synth-drenched arrangements, yet the combination still retained a visceral power that left no question about Art's punk pedigree. That was most evident on the jagged "My Empty House," a glimpse into domestic turmoil made all the more horrific by a video created with the help of several favours from Vancouver's Bridge Studios, soon to be one of the city's leading film and television facilities. The starkly lit, post-apocalyptic set perfectly jelled with the sound, and the video rightly earned regular play on MuchMusic.

"As a band, we were in the songs," Fulber explained. "The drama was created by the band's lifestyle, the drug use, and the relationships. So when Art came up with a song, we all knew what he was talking about." That further played out soon after the sessions were completed, when Gord Nicholl discovered that his girlfriend Tami Thirlwell was now in a relationship with Art, prompting him to abruptly leave the band. Fortunately, Fulber had a replacement waiting in the wings in Susann Richter, who, on top of her law degree and a master's in microbiology, was also an accomplished keyboardist and harmony singer. Being as well read as Art, her full-time presence immediately altered the band's dynamic, and Art welcomed her opinion on his lyrics.

As 1987 unfolded, the now-stable Poisoned lineup consisting of Art, Fulber, Richter, and Little continued expanding their repertoire of original material, and they headed back into Mushroom Studios for more demo sessions, this time overseen by engineer Rolf Hennemann, known for his work on Heart's early albums, when that band was based in Vancouver during the mid-'70s. "With that stuff, we produced it as a band," Fulber said. "We laid the tracks down basically live off the floor, and Art recorded his vocals later, with Susann overdubbing some backups. Taylor came up with his own drum parts, and everyone felt really good about the results. One of the reasons we recorded the second batch at Mushroom was because Rolf Hennemann worked there, and he could really record guitars. And then Bob Rock mixed it during his downtime at Little Mountain for a few cases of beer. I thought it sounded great, but I was the one who paid for it."

Rock's ongoing support was indeed growing valuable now that his partnership with producer Bruce Fairbairn was yielding multi-platinum results. Their efforts on Bon Jovi's *Slippery When Wet* in particular had put Little Mountain on the map, and by the end of 1987 both Rock and Fairbairn would enter the rarefied strata of internationally known producers after raising Aerosmith from the dead with the album *Permanent Vacation*. Still, Fulber's further attempt to find a record deal in Los Angeles came up empty, in all likelihood simply because of the band's name. In 1986, the LA–based glam-metal band Poison scored a surprise hit with its debut album, *Look What the Cat Dragged In*. The group's outlandish, heavily made-up image made it one of the easiest targets for the ridicule of anyone in the emerging "alternative rock" community, a problem Art could never have foreseen. But with Poison's videos in heavy rotation on both MTV and MuchMusic, it made little sense for Art to continue working under the name "Poisoned." If these songs were going to be Art's best shot at fulfilling all the promise of the previous decade, then the best option was to record and release them under his own name.

CHAPTER 7

A Pretty Dangerous Game

ONE DAY IN 1987, Sam Feldman's receptionist buzzed to say that Art Bergmann was here to see him. There was no meeting scheduled, as far as Sam knew, and besides, what would an old punk rocker—which was essentially all the name "Art Bergmann" meant to Sam—want with him?

"Art walks in, unannounced, and says, 'I've got this song that we've made a video for,'" Feldman recounted. "So I said, 'Okay, leave it with me, I'll take a listen to it.' He said, 'Okay,' and walked out. He seemed very shy. Of course, whatever format the video was on wouldn't play, so I had to call him and have him bring it in again. When I finally heard the song, I loved it, and when Art said he needed some help, I said, 'No problem, I'll be your manager.'"

With that simple agreement, Feldman plunged himself into a world of which he had little experience up until then. By the time he'd turned twenty in the late 1960s, Feldman was determined to get involved in the music business, and got a chance after landing a job as the doorman at a Vancouver club called the Daisy. It was one of the many rooms in town to which Bruce Allen held exclusive rights, and Feldman quickly became attuned to how the booking process worked. Within weeks, he was helping set up gigs for his friend Harry Kalensky's blues-rock band Uncle Slug—a few of whose members would later form the quirky pop-soul band Doug & the Slugs—and found himself on Bruce Allen's radar as an up-and-coming local artist manager who could potentially assist with running his rapidly expanding business.

"Bruce, at that time, was twenty-four years old, so he was like the old guy, establishment," Feldman said. "I had a meeting with Bruce at the Mayfair Towers, and he made me a funny kind of offer, which was 'We'll split the money and I'll pay all the expenses out of my half.' I said, 'I'm not doing that deal because in three weeks you'll realize how stupid it is and it will be all over.' My proposal was to pay the bands first and then split the rest. We shook on that and became partners."

That partnership flourished over the coming decade, and in 1987 Feldman's main responsibility was still to handle bookings for Allen's top clients, Bryan Adams and Loverboy. However, he balanced that work with his own modest stable of management clients, composed of his old friends in Doug & the Slugs (for whom Feldman had mortgaged his home to pay for the recording of their 1980 debut album *Cognac and Bologna*), along with arena rockers Trooper and the Headpins, whose uncomplicated records were eagerly devoured by Canadian commercial-radio programmers seeking homegrown content.

Art represented something entirely different. Even though Feldman was captivated by the Poisoned demos, he also understood they would be a tougher sell than what he was accustomed to. Ray Fulber had already approached Bruce Allen about a management deal, and although Allen said he loved the tapes, he still hadn't erased the memory of his lone meeting with the Young Canadians. Allen instead made an offer to represent Bob Rock as a producer, based on the Poisoned demos.

That bad blood between Art and his business partner didn't matter to Feldman, but even his own reputation couldn't overcome some initial obstacles. "I couldn't get Art a deal anywhere," Feldman said. "I had been making large deals with big companies, and Art's songs were just too alternative at the time, at least for the people at those labels. That's how I ended up at Duke Street Records, which was a little label distributed by PolyGram, back in the days when there was an actual record business."

Andy Hermant, one of Toronto's leading recording studio builders, launched Duke Street in 1984 as an extension of his production activities at Manta Sound, the studio he'd opened in 1971. It gained a reputation out of the gate through A Foot in Coldwater's hit "(Make Me Do) Anything You Want" and in short order became a studio of choice for Bruce Cockburn, Rough Trade, and Bryan Adams, as well as many US and European rock acts seeking a more affordable place to work. In creating Duke Street Records, Hermant struck a partnership with WEA (Warner) Music—before moving to MCA/PolyGram in 1986—with the intent to serve as a quasi–farm system for developing new artists who would eventually move up to the major label. It was a novel idea that was gaining traction in the US music industry, where labels such as Sire, I.R.S., Slash, and Enigma had become hugely influential in ushering "underground" artists into the mainstream. The artist on whom Duke Street placed its biggest bet was Jane Siberry, a former folksinger whose sound had evolved, through the implementation of cutting-edge digital technology, into a distinct blend of pop and performance art previously attempted by Kate Bush and Laurie Anderson. Siberry's 1984 album *No Borders Here* had a profound impact on many musicians, particularly in Toronto's emerging "alternative" scene, and once MuchMusic put the video for the quirky single "Mimi on the Beach" into rotation, it helped push sales of *No Borders Here* to forty thousand, a resounding success for a previously unknown Canadian artist.

Duke Street signed on to do more experimental projects over the next two years, including albums by the innovative Toronto prog/new-wave band FM (featuring Nash the Slash) and newcomers Chalk Circle, whose approach was in line with bands like U2, Echo & the Bunnymen, and others refining post-punk into something more closely resembling traditional rock and roll. For Art, the environment was still a far cry from the beer-soaked mayhem of the Smilin' Buddha, but now that he was well into his thirties, it presented an opportunity to finally make a mark on the national stage. "I was trying to have realistic expectations," Feldman said. "Whether [Poisoned] wanted to be presented as a band, in my mind I was managing Art because he was obviously the focus. The motivation behind making the deal was really just to give Art a chance to step up to the plate, because I knew there were other things that were going to present a challenge, specifically the drug use."

That turned out not to be of great concern to Duke Street's vice-president, Adrian Heaps, a year younger than Art and the member of the organization most enthusiastic about adding him to the roster. Heaps's attitude didn't change despite the embarrassment of watching the band get thrown out of the Rivoli in Toronto during the contract-signing meeting for being drunk and disruptive. Heaps had arranged the Toronto jaunt in order to finalize the deal, and to allow the band to plan recording sessions that would take place at Manta Sound. It had been widely assumed that Bob Rock would produce the album, but that plan was quickly altered when word came from Vancouver that John Cale had heard some of the Poisoned demos, loved them, and was interested in working with the band.

Cale was the Welsh-born, classically trained co-founder of the Velvet Underground who had put his production stamp on other era-defining albums, such as the Stooges' self-titled debut and Patti Smith's *Horses*. Despite this, his life and career since leaving the VU in 1968 had gone through several peaks and valleys due to his own addictions and uncompromising creative vision. Yet that history only enhanced his image as one of punk rock's true founding figures. Thinking back to the first time he'd heard the Velvet Underground's "Heroin"—its otherworldly sound driven by Cale's droning viola—Art became consumed by the possibility of working with one of the few people he considered a genuine inspiration.

Cale, at that point, was in the midst of putting his life back in order after spending several years in the grip of alcoholism and cocaine addiction. His attempts to make commercially accessible solo albums during the first half of the 1980s had proved fruitless, but he remained grounded through his marriage to actress Risé Irushalmi, who bore him a daughter in 1985. Becoming a father for the first time proved to be the motivation Cale needed to get completely clean, and for the next several years he balanced his home life with composing classical pieces while earning steady income through production work.

Cale was lured to Vancouver to hear the Scramblers, a new band Bruce Allen was managing composed of punk veterans, including charismatic frontman Howard Rix and guitarist Ziggy Sigmund, formerly with the Vancouver scene's infamous proto-grunge band Slow. Allen's choice to tap the Scramblers rather than Poisoned as his entry into the emerging world of alternative rock suggested he'd already formulated a plan, and his desire for full control of the process manifested itself further when he set up a new label, Penta Entertainment, specifically for the Scramblers, which would be distributed in the US by Elektra Records. The hope was that Cale would recreate the same magic with the Scramblers that he'd conjured in the studio for the Stooges, who'd signed with Elektra in 1968 Yet, despite the brief hype surrounding the Scramblers, it was soon apparent that Allen was never fully committed to the project, leaving any long-term plans for them in limbo. For his part, Cale liked the band, but during his visit to Vancouver he ended up only mixing some tracks they had already recorded. Without any clear direction, the proposed Scramblers album was ultimately shelved entirely.

Still, Cale's trip proved worthwhile when someone slipped him a copy of the Poisoned tape. As Ray Fulber recalled, "Apparently, Cale listened to it while he was on the way to the airport,

Early solo promotional photo.
(Alex Waterhouse-Hayward)

and when he got back to New York, he called Sam Feldman and said he'd work with us."

While the news of Cale's participation was, on the surface, a cause for celebration, it wasn't treated as such by everyone, specifically those actually making the music. According to Fulber, "Bob Rock was in a strip club when someone told him that he wasn't going to be producing Art's new album, and he was so pissed off that he went into the bathroom and didn't come out for half an hour. Bob was such a big fan of Art's that he felt completely snubbed. I remember Bob saying while he was mixing those demos, 'Wait until we get in there and really do it.' I mean, he had it all thought out, how he was going to make the record he'd always wanted Art to make. I'd spent around $60 or $80,000 up to that point on the assumption that Bob was going to be our producer, and I couldn't help feeling like this was a betrayal after all that Bob had done."

I never fought for [Cale] to be the producer. I desperately wanted Bob Rock. But Sam thought he would make things sound too "homogenized." I couldn't believe it. Fuck, that was the biggest mistake. The whole session, I wanted to slash my wrists.

In early 1988, Art, Fulber, Richter, and Little flew from Vancouver to Toronto, with Cale and his trusted engineer Roger Moutenot flying in from New York. But any sense of excitement was quashed when it became obvious that the band's lifestyle clashed with Cale's new-found commitment to sobriety. Furthermore, Fulber remained furious over recording new versions of songs he believed had been perfectly captured in Rock's mixes. "It was chaos," Fulber admitted. "We would be trying to work something out musically, and Cale would be in the booth reading a newspaper. He did really like Susann's keyboard playing, but that only caused him to put more focus on her at the expense of Art's guitar playing. At one point I went psychotic and got into a physical confrontation with the engineer. I think I had him in a headlock under the mixing board."

Moutenot, who had experience in the studio with Lou Reed, recognized a similar lyrical quality in Art's songs, and had his own vision of how the sessions would unfold, based on his prior collaborations with Cale. "I was really excited to work at Manta Sound, but my first impression of the main room was how dead it sounded, like it was built specifically to record strings," Moutenot said. "My first memory of the sessions is actually seeing John taking away cymbals and toms from the drum kit until it was just bare bones. John didn't like cymbals; that was just part of his sound. The drummer, Taylor, was asking, 'You want me to play with this?' That kind of set the tone of everyone questioning John's decisions."

Nonetheless, Moutenot said he got along well with everyone in the band once they all had a chance to settle in after the first couple of days. "I don't think there were any secrets about the drug use going on in that band, and there were initially some strange vibes in the air. I think they were conscious of keeping that hidden from John, because they knew he'd sobered up. After the third day, I went out for drinks with the band and that's when they explained to me what was going on, and then suddenly it all made sense. But it created a weird dynamic throughout the making of that record. John had seen everything over the course of his career, though, so I'm sure he knew what was going on."

Moutenot had his own first-hand experience of dealing with Cale's cleanliness, noting one instance when the producer unleashed his wrath on him for coming into the booth smelling like cigarette smoke. On the other hand, Cale constantly irritated the musicians with the amount of attention he appeared to be giving to his squash game, rather than to the task at hand. Still, the producer retained full control, putting his personal brand on the new version of "My Empty House" that opened the album. The differences between the two recordings were most obvious in each one's individual feel: the Bob Rock mix had captured a road-hardened band playing at full tilt, while the Cale version sounded stiff, almost bordering on mechanical. Although Art once again delivered a ferocious reading of the confession of a man pushed to the brink of killing his wife, and capped it off with a majestically unhinged guitar solo, the washes of synthesizers throughout the rest of the new take invariably tied the song to a 1980s production aesthetic that was already becoming obsolete.

It seemed an unusual approach for Cale to take. As an artist hailed for almost single-handedly introducing avant-garde elements to rock and roll, the notion of him trying to make Art Bergmann "radio friendly" was, on the surface, absurd. Yet, in an era dominated by over-the-top heavy metal bands and artists from the 1960s finally figuring out how to market themselves to a new generation, what lay on the surface was more critical than ever, particularly for artists trying to get a meaningful message across. In 1987, the singer-songwriter Suzanne Vega scored a surprise pop hit with "Luka," sung from the perspective of an abused child, and one of the biggest songs of 1988 would be Tracy Chapman's "Fast Car," a stark ballad about a young couple trying to escape the life of grinding poverty that had destroyed their families. Both songs found audiences on their melodic strength, and perhaps based on that reasoning, it was decided to give extra attention to Art's "Our Little Secret" as the album's projected first single.

If its title alone wasn't an indication, from the opening lines "I know what she wants but she don't get it from me, opened up an broken by the age of thirteen," it was clear the song was about incest. Yet Art took on the subject without his usual cynicism, instead revealing a previously untapped well of empathy that made a verse such as "Daddy read a lot but he never took us anywhere, just a room with a lock at the top of the stairs" all the more devastating. Cale must have sensed that too, and in giving "Our Little Secret" the full '80s production treatment he suddenly put Art's work into an entirely new context. Art's following of hardcore punks and rockers could complain all they wanted about the synthesizers and intrusive backing choruses, but none of that could cancel out his sincerity as a songwriter.

Conversely, Cale and Art shared a similar black humour, a connection that helped shape "Final Cliche," written as a true—and highly detailed—account of his old Mount Lehman LSD supplier Danny Clark's suicide. From a lyrical perspective, Art essentially just reported the facts, but Cale's push to turn it into a bouncy pop song, complete with Susann Richter's "Oh-oh-oh" backing vocals, showed the extent he was willing to go to make Art's dark visions commercially palatable. It could also be said that both Cale and Art wove masochistic tendencies into their work, perhaps as a by-product of addiction. Nowhere was that more evident than on what would become the album's title track, "Crawl with Me," with the narrator offering a dire warning to a potential partner that "If we fall in love, it will be your living end."

Cale said, after the album was completed, "There is a strong streak of humanity in what [Art] was singing about. There's a depth there, something that will give him longevity." Still, if Cale's ultimate goal was to present the full range of Art's writing, he had once again fallen short with other songs from the Poisoned catalogue, like "Charity" and "Runaway Train," on which Art chronicled the street life that was inextricably tied to the punk rock community. Another in that group was "The Junkie Don't Care," a terrifying portrait of a teenage girl drawn into a life of prostitution, whose enabler could have been Art's own impression of himself. As with the new "My Empty House," the song's overall power was dampened by a rigid arrangement that siphoned out the humanity Cale had praised, precisely when it was most needed. While Cale did complete the job he was hired to do, in the view of those directly involved, the album's shortcomings vastly outweighed the benefits of having his name attached to it.

"From my recollection, the sessions were fast and furious, probably about two weeks in total," Moutenot said. "There were times when we'd be overdubbing one of Art's guitar solos and I'd want to do another take, but John would say, 'No, that's good.' There were a few instances like that where it felt like we could push things a bit further, but then there would be a quick decision to move on to something else."

> I should have known by [Cale's] aloofness that he was the wrong choice, but the guy's one of my all-time idols. The guy's done amazing work, but he was on [anti-alcoholism drug] Antabuse and playing squash at 6 o'clock every day while I was trying to do the album. I gave up in disgust and that's why that album has no guitar on it. People love that album, and it brought the songs out, but so what? All this tinkly keyboard shit all over it—we had to nip that in the bud.

The idol worship had long worn off by the time the album was mixed, and according to Fulber, no one was in the mood to listen to it. "I was having a complete mental breakdown from my drug use. I was hospitalized slightly just before we went out there to record, and I was in very serious post-cocaine psychosis, so there was a lot of insanity and everything. The night we got the mixes, we took the truck that Duke Street or Sam had rented for us, got onto the

401, slapped in the tape, and cranked it up. I think we were about two songs into it—I was driving, Art was in the passenger seat—and I looked over and I saw tears rolling down his cheek. Like, he knew. We knew. But by that time, the money was spent, and we kind of had to go into denial."

Crawl with Me, the first release under Art's own name, arrived in stores across Canada on July 5, 1988. With funding from VideoFACT, the grant body set up by MuchMusic in 1984 to help keep it supplied with Canadian content, Duke Street was able to pay for a video for "Our Little Secret," created by James O'Mara and Kate Ryan. The concept was straightforward, showing Art in a blank room containing only a chair. He wore the street-poet garb of ratty white T-shirt, tight black jeans, and boots, and lip-synched while tousling his shaggy blond hair and improvising moves that suggested how vulnerable he felt, alone in front of the camera. Those sequences were interspersed with shots of an empty suburban neighbourhood that did manage to capture the sense of isolation and abandonment inherent to the song. In all, the video was a strange and unlikely introduction to Art's music for kids across Canada, and most radio programmers were unsure of what to do with the song as well, especially those concerned about its theme.

> Interview with the *Vancouver Sun*, July 9, 1988:
> ["Our Little Secret"] is kind of weird because it's like a brother talking to his sister about his secret, and they're lovers or something. That's how I figured it out, anyway. Checking out the limits of human behaviour is a pretty dangerous game. Flirting with insanity, flirting with dangerous, slimy people just for something to write about—I sometimes feel like I'm using people, using people's deaths for a song. I was like in a tunnel, digging the wrong way. The songs were, 'What can I write about now? Ah, here's one, further, further somewhere left of nihilism.' I think everybody thinks about [death] every day. Dying. Worms. I've chosen life. Remember that great scene in *Under The Volcano* with Albert Finney? 'I choose hell!' God, that's scary. It all sort of came to a head with this album. People convinced me that I don't need to live the way I lived for a long time anymore, waking me up. I had sort of hit the wall, hit the bottom trying to make this record. I realized that I've got enough material to last me the rest of my life. I don't have to feel like I have to have a nervous breakdown on tape. The cynicism in my marrow was pretty volatile. I feel pretty good about myself now. I'm actually almost happy.

Another video was made for "Final Cliche," this one showing the entire band miming to the track on a dramatically lit set. Particular focus was placed on Susann Richter, and her presence made for an interesting visual contrast to the vast majority of videos, in which women were largely resigned to the role of sex objects. It also gave audiences a sample of how the band would present itself live. Feldman had booked a cross-Canada tour that kicked off mid-August in Calgary, with a showcase at Lee's Palace in Toronto on September 7 as the centrepiece. Following that was a run of dates opening for 54-40, still touring in support of its hugely successful album *Show Me*, containing the hits "One Day in Your Life" and "One Gun."

"We were treated really well by Sam," Fulber said. "He got Doug & the Slugs' crew to go out with us, which was great for me because I could have new strings on my bass every night. We started off playing universities, but pretty soon we were doing shows on our own."

Feldman had gone above and beyond to invite all of his industry contacts to the Lee's Palace gig, and even flew in from Vancouver himself to make sure all was going smoothly. Needless to say, he was a little surprised at what he saw. "Every detail in those days was so important in terms of getting the tastemakers and influencers on your side, and I was doing everything I could for that show," he said. "Then I go out to the bus and Art's there passed out, and not because he was taking a nap. I don't know if I said it to him at that moment, but I do remember saying to him, 'I don't give a shit what you do, I don't care if you fuck sheep. If it starts to hurt you, that's your business, but if it affects me, I have to say something. That stuff just leads to problems like crossing the border, and other people in the industry shying away from you.' I mean, who was going to gamble resources on a guy who was going to be unreliable? So, for sure, the drug use, which again wasn't a secret, presented some challenges."

Future CBC Radio producer Chris Wodskou saw one of the 54-40 shows the following week at the University of Waterloo's Fed Hall and picked up on some of that too, writing scathingly in the campus newspaper *Imprint*, "If facial lines could talk, the weathered faces of Art and his bassist could provide enough sordid memoirs to fill a Jackie Collins trilogy... Maybe there were too many French braids and Roots sweatshirts around the audience for a hard-nosed, working-class stiff like Art, but his obnoxious stage manner didn't make a whole posse of friends. Just play your songs and quit being such a miserable bastard and maybe you'll get somewhere, Art."

Bidding adieu to 1988.

The tour carried on into autumn, even though by then *Crawl with Me* had fallen off the national album chart, as compiled by *RPM* magazine. In interviews with that publication and others, Art was careful not to disparage Cale's work, but had already made up his mind to not repeat the mistakes he believed had stifled the album's potential reach.

Interview with the Toronto *Star*, September 2, 1988:
I like [*Crawl with Me*]... In hindsight, I like it. But at first I was shocked, to tell you the truth. It was so clear! But Duke Street has given us a full commitment for at least three albums. If the first one doesn't sell, they're not going to throw you on a shelf and just write you off.

A Never-Was
Trying to Be a Has-Been

By spring 1989, *Crawl with Me* had sold about 20,000 copies—hardly a failure, but only half-way to meeting the threshold for gold certification in Canada. Still, having the clout of some influential industry figures in his corner earned Art two Juno Award nominations, one for best video—which technically went to "Our Little Secret" directors James O'Mara and Kate Ryan—and one for most promising male vocalist. Keen observers of Canadian music could often find reason to question each of the Junos' "most promising" categories, given that they didn't recognize artists who hadn't graduated to major-label status. Art's inclusion a decade into his recording career seemed particularly bizarre to his hard-core following, but at the same time it was a sign of the changes that had slowly developed on the national scene since the last Juno Awards ceremony had taken place, in November 1987.

One of the big winners in 1989 was Blue Rodeo, a scrappy group of experienced Toronto musicians who fused the novel term *roots rock* and psychedelia into a sound that built on the foundation Handsome Ned had partially laid in the vibrant Queen Street West club scene. Blue Rodeo's debut album, *Outskirts*, was a triumph in both style and substance, and for the televised Juno gala held on March 12 at Toronto's O'Keefe Centre, producers capitalized on a passing-of-the-torch moment by getting several Blue Rodeo members to support a performance by the surviving Canadian members of the Band, that year's Canadian Music Hall of Fame inductees. The Band's de facto leader, Robbie Robertson, was also a main attraction, picking up several awards for his debut solo album, made in collaboration with Daniel Lanois, another figure who, like Art, had long worked outside of Canada's music-business establishment before emerging as one of the most significant record producers of the decade.

That year's most-promising-group category also served as a bellwether indicating that a new generation of bands was coming to replace the old guard of '70s holdovers and challenge those at the top of the Canadian pop food chain. There was little dispute that 54-40 had earned its nomination, and the same could be said of the Pursuit of Happiness, led by one-time Edmonton punk Moe Berg, whose caustic lyricism and devotion to power-pop songcraft had attracted the admiration of Todd Rundgren, who produced the band's widely praised debut album *Love Junk*.

Art's competition for most promising male vocalist included his Toronto peer Andrew Cash, who, following the breakup of L'Etranger, became the first Canadian artist signed to Britain's prestigious Island Records. Yet the status quo was largely maintained, with the most-promising-male-vocalist Juno ultimately going to Colin James, a blues-guitar prodigy who had been mentored by Stevie Ray Vaughan.

Sam Feldman had booked Art on another cross-Canada tour to coincide with Juno festivities, which Art agreed to attend on his best behaviour, if for no other reason than to provide some west coast representation in the face of the Toronto-centric crowd. At the same time, Art had to admit that the nomination was affecting how he was now perceived.

Interview with the *Toronto Star*, March 10, 1989:
It's so weird. I was just in Winnipeg, and all these people are so friendly now—radio stations that used to hang up when I called. I like the word "Promising" because it keeps you young.

Before packing away his false front and leaving Toronto, Art made a point of checking in with some acquaintances, both older and more recent. One in particular was living in the city's low-rent Kensington Market neighbourhood, where Art found him in the midst of severe cocaine withdrawal. He was hallucinating, convinced that every Black person he saw was a past connection that had ripped him off, and babbling incoherently about killing them all. Art did what he could to defuse the situation, but in the aftermath it brought into clearer focus the theme he had been envisioning for his next collection of songs, an unflinching exploration of a society in decline, circa 1989, with guitars restored.

The Kensington incident became "Dirge No. 1," which on paper stood on its own as a spoken-word piece, with images of chicken blood running in the gutters, and the constant throb of Black dance music blasting out of shops bringing twisted, racist thoughts to a boil in the mind of the song's subject. Art captured the entire experience in graphic detail: "So he took his favourite red knife / Stuck it in some dealer's thigh / Took all his dope / What a mess, my my / He came back up to our flat / Pulled a dirty fit out of the garbage / Came into my room, he said 'You gotta help me' / I said 'Hello you old devil' / And smashed him right in the teeth."

The story told in "Dirge No. 1" culminated in a faint hope of redemption, not only for its main character, but for anyone else who had sacrificed their sanity to addiction. Ray Fulber believed the notion of redemption came from an entirely different source. "Susann's father was a painter, and he would make money selling these pictures of Christ that he would turn out almost like an assembly line. We had one nailed to the wall in my studio, so it was a constant presence."

Fulber added that late spring and early summer 1989 was the period when the band, now known as the Showdogs, was most cohesive. Although that provided a creative advantage, it also exacerbated the drug dependency, given that Fulber had a steady supply of heroin coming from friends in Shanghai and northern Thailand. "We did a lot of writing as a band during that time that produced a lot of great songs," Fulber said. "We were getting together at my place basically five days a week and jamming out ideas, but at the same time, Art and I especially were really fucked up. The songs were a reflection of the society around the band, and every-thing Art wrote was based in that reality. A lot of people around us were dying or getting themselves into deep trouble."

Indeed, the songs that were emerging painted a dark, terrifying picture of relationships formed around addiction, with the spectre of death always hovering nearby. On the minor-key, Iggy Pop–esque rocker "Bar of Pain," vulnerability inevitably led to betrayal: "There's damage in your eye / There's damage in your smile / Reflections in my golden drink / Reflections in your golden eye." It ended with one of Art's more memorable images, simultaneously absurd and tragic: "Looking and looking into each other's eyes / Just a couple of flies on a lonely cowpie."

On the ballad "More Blue Shock," Art expounded on an acquaintance's downward spiral after being charged with assault and winding up helpless to do anything about it. "It reminded me of a friend / They found him hanging from a light fixture in the middle of his room just before breakfast / Swinging in the gloom / And I couldn't help thinking this was gonna hap-pen to you / All screwed up in your head in your cell / Swinging in the gloom."

Yet Art didn't let himself off the hook in many of the lyrics, particularly "Hospital Song," a virtual blow-by-blow account of a relationship that ended in nearly the direst possible cir-cumstances. Beginning with an acknowledgement of culpability, he sang in a breezy, Ray Davies–like manner: "I watch you sleep in your tubes and IVs / They kept your face so clean / Would it seem too mean / To pull the plug on your dream machine / Would I be losing you or would we meet again." Adding to the song's overall perversity was the chorus: "Maybe later we'll get together and have a relapse."

> Interview with the *Vancouver Sun*, May 24, 1990:
> I got this girl in deep, deep trouble one time. She came in a cab, left in an ambulance. Everything is true. We're makin' movies here! [But] to me, I'm just another stand-up comedian. The jokes—some of them just go "fwooom" over people's heads. Some people take everything so goddamn literally. I'm in a really stupid business. People are so scared these days. Everybody goes, 'It's so alternative.' Whatever happened to Jim Morrison and Jimi Hendrix and John Lennon? The music of '65 and '66 when radio was great—it was mean and nasty, coming out of garages.

Art channelled that idea into the fiercest rocker among the new material. Built around a savage, slashing guitar riff, "Bound for Vegas" took direct aim at some of the sacred cows of his youth now pandering to their grown-up fanbases that had cashed in their ideals during the 1980s. "It's in my heart / I'm making a financial start / I'm a never-was trying to be a has-been / A has-been on the comeback trail." Art spat out those words with a certain degree of irony, but there was no questioning the visceral appeal of the music.

As the new material steadily coalesced, everyone close to Art was chomping at the bit to rectify the missteps of *Crawl with Me*, among them a new face on the scene, Jeff Rogers, manager of the Pursuit of Happiness. "My friends Allen Moy and Keith Porteous, who managed 54-40, made me aware of Art when *Crawl with Me* came out and that really got me into his music," Rogers said. "I was good friends with Sam Feldman too, and when I found out he was managing Art, I called him up and just suggested that we manage him together. Sam loved Art and really believed in him, but I think he was happy that someone was offering some help. Neither Sam nor I were under any illusions that we were going to make a lot of money from Art, but we both wanted him to reach an audience that would appreciate his work as much as we did."

It was also of great benefit that Rogers managed producer Chris Wardman, who became the ideal candidate to keep all parties happy in light of the Cale experience. Wardman had come up through the Toronto post-punk scene, attaining early notoriety as guitarist and songwriter in Blue Peter, which reached its commercial peak in 1983 with the album *Falling* and the hit "Don't Walk Past." Wardman's interest in production was fully stoked during the making of *Falling* with British producer Steve Nye, whose credits included Bryan Ferry and the Cure, and Wardman moved into production full-time following Blue Peter's breakup in 1985. He became involved with Duke Street through working with its artists Chalk Circle and Neo A4, and although his track record suggested a new-wave aesthetic that wouldn't jibe with Art's philosophy, the soft-spoken Wardman immediately grasped the parameters of the job.

"The label's head of A&R, Adrian Heaps, played me a cassette of the Bob Rock demos, and they were awesome," Wardman said. "That made me aware of Art, and then when I listened to *Crawl with Me*, I was slightly disappointed, as I guess he was too. So my main job was to fix the lack of guitars."

In order to get the raw sound everyone was demanding, it was agreed to make some modifications to Profile Studios in Vancouver, where the sessions were slated to take place. Wardman, Fulber, and Art duly went to Sam Feldman with a shopping list for plywood and concrete, and received the response "Are you making a record or building a barn?" Once the pieces were in place, it became a matter of capturing the right atmosphere for each song.

"'Bound for Vegas' was a pretty easy one to lay down because it was such a great, straight-up rock song," Wardman said. "One of the amps Art was using was a vintage Vox that sounded incredible. We were going to double-track some of his parts, but midway through one of those takes the amp blew up. From then on, our slogan became 'Everything sounds amazing until it blows up.' I do remember having to coax Art a bit to record 'More Blue Shock.' I think he was a little too close to what that one was about. For 'Dirge No. 1,' though, I had some involvement in the arrangement. The story that song told was also really heavy, so I thought the music should reflect that. There was a cinematic quality to the words as well, and that put me in the mind of Led Zeppelin's 'Kashmir.' I don't recall anyone really objecting to that. We did a lot of pre-production work and rehearsals, so the actual recording went pretty efficiently. The album was done in about a couple weeks. I think the entire band had been wounded after working with John Cale, so when they sensed that I was on their wavelength, we created a pretty good chemistry."

Recording *Sexual Roulette*, Profile Studios 1989. (COURTESY CHRIS WARDMAN)

> I hate the whole recording process; it's like making me go inside out or something. The thing is, you can record in any studio, in your living room, as long as you've got a good engineer who knows what he's doing. Make the songs go on tape as loud as possible, and then make them claw their way through the speakers.

The track that ultimately tied the album together was "Sexual Roulette," a scathing observation that the concept of free love pervasive in the 1960s and '70s had descended into a true gamble with people's lives, from both a mental and a physical standpoint. An obvious parallel was that by 1989, HIV-AIDS had become a part of mainstream consciousness, with the number of reported cases in the US reaching a hundred thousand that year as a combined result of unprotected sex and intravenous drug use. Art drew from those around him facing what seemed like an inevitable fate, writing, "This is my body, I'm doing time / Are you giving me something I'll get in five years' time?"

But the ideas in "Sexual Roulette" delved deeper into the psyches of those whose toxic relationships set them on a path where a disease was not necessarily required to end their lives. These were the people whose simple desire for love left them as easy prey for anyone desiring to exploit them. In that sense, Art demonstrated once again that he was capable of setting aside his cynicism to reveal his deep well of empathy.

> There's a bit of autobiography there, although you'd have to take the songs line by line. Sometimes I'll make up a character or play someone I know. And obviously, things have to be embellished a bit. But the nastiest bits are usually true.

Interview with the *Calgary Herald*, May 17, 1990:
If I wasn't in music, I probably would be into some weird form of terrorism or something. One of the most lasting images of the 20th Century will be the Holocaust, and it bugs me every day just to feel I'm related to those people who did that. It just overwhelms me; I just don't know how or why anyone could do that to somebody else. But you gotta face facts sooner or later, and the basic fact is death for all of us. I think it's something everybody thinks about. And personally I think there's a lot of humour there, when you face these facts and learn to laugh at them. Down at the bottom, things are really black and white. People have to do certain things to survive, like the guy from "My Empty House." He shoots his family, you know, and I find it much more interesting than a basic love song that's been written 40 times. Rock and roll, for me, is like a big battle between good and evil, and that's the way it should be.

In keeping with Art's perspective on mortality, there was an unsettling thank you to Tami Thirlwell buried in the album's credits. His relationship with her had grown so important to his well-being that Art chose for the album cover a James O'Mara photo that captured both of them in a stark black-and-white shot, displaying Art in classic French *nouvelle vague* style, mid–cigarette drag, and Tami in profile, wearing a bolero hat and facing in the opposite direction with eyes cast down. Nothing about the pose suggested any relationship between them, apart from their individual inner turmoil at finding themselves in this situation together.

Although *Sexual Roulette* was completed by autumn 1989, Duke Street held off on releasing it until March 1990, partly to set up a potentially busy summer touring schedule. An outtake from the sessions, the politically charged rocker "War Party," appeared at the same time on the soundtrack to the independent film *Terminal City Ricochet*, a dystopian satire that starred Jello Biafra and Joe Keithley. But in the interim, Art mainly occupied his time in revisiting the fuck-band concept by playing guitar with Evil Twang, a loose conglomeration composed of various Vancouver scene notables and fronted by Chris Houston, founding member of Hamilton, Ontario, punk outfit the Forgotten Rebels, and responsible for the band's signature song, "Surfin' on Heroin."

Houston had relocated to Vancouver to work as a writer on a CBC television project, but also for a change of musical scenery. Along with recharging his own batteries, Evil Twang served to energize many of his friends as well. "That band was a lot of fun," Houston said. "I sort of imagined it as something like Johnny Thunders and the Heartbreakers, and it was a great privilege to play with all those musicians. It was always a topic of conversation that people like Art weren't getting the recognition they deserved, but it still felt like a magic time, and we ended up being able to draw 850 people at the Commodore."

In between gigs, recording sessions were set up with Cec English at Profile, where Art contributed stinging guitar parts to the '60s-garage-rock-inspired "Just Once for Kicks" and a new, explosive version of "Surfin' on Heroin." "It was an exciting time," Houston added. "I got the sense that there was a real community in Vancouver, where people supported each other."

Evil Twang provided Art with a welcome distraction as a new decade beckoned, and as those behind the scenes aimed to position him within the rapidly changing landscape of Canadian rock. The most obvious sign of those changes was evident at the 1990 Juno Awards, held on March 18 in Toronto, when the most-promising-group honour was given to the Tragically Hip, the one-time bar band from Kingston, Ontario, which, from the moment it released its eponymous debut EP late in 1987, captured the hearts of the nation with lead vocalist Gord Downie's poetic flights and riveting onstage persona. The Hip's 1989 full-length debut album *Up to Here* was an instant hit, winning over the remaining few who had refused to believe that homegrown artists could produce authentic rock and roll that reflected their upbringing, as bands in other parts of the world appeared to do effortlessly. The icing on the cake was that the Hip, the Pursuit of Happiness, and other bands of their ilk were no longer being ignored by American labels, and with *Sexual Roulette*, Art seemed well positioned to join that club.

"My main thought at that time was I needed to get Art a record deal," Rogers said. "My feeling was 'Here's the greatest living treasure in Canadian music, and he's all mine to talk about.' So that's what I did, and there was definitely interest, especially from Kate Hyman at Chrysalis Records. Kate had signed the Pursuit of Happiness, so I had a great relationship with her, and when Chris Wardman played me *Sexual Roulette*, I felt confident right away in telling her that this could do just as well or even better than TPOH. So I invited Kate to come up to Vancouver to see Art play at 86 Street Music Hall, and he came out wearing this kind of blouse-y, pirate-y shirt and just killed. It was an amazing night, Kate loved him, we all had a good time, and then we ended up at my favourite Chinese restaurant in the Marine Building. I'd made friends with a waiter there and he let us go upstairs into the secret mah-jong room—everything seemed to be going according to plan. Having Sam and I co-managing Art really should have meant we were unstoppable, but Kate didn't end up signing Art and I really don't know why. It was one of those things that just left us all kind of baffled."

One reason might have been Art's behaviour at the time, which could verge on belligerent when he was drinking. That was revealed when Feldman once again urged Art to attend the Juno ceremonies in order to do some personal promotion to mark *Sexual Roulette*'s Canadian release. This time, without a nomination at stake, Art was under no constraints when it came to being a fly in the ointment. His friend John Mackie, on assignment to cover the Junos for the *Vancouver Sun*, knew Art would be the life of the party and stayed close to cover the action. "At a Blue Rodeo showcase," Mackie said, "he leapt up onstage, screamed, 'One fucking chord!' and led the band through a 'spontaneous' rap song before falling over. After he left the stage, he tried to show his appreciation by throwing a flower to the band. Problem was, he tried to yank one out of a plastic flower arrangement and wound up splattering the flowers and the planter in which they sat all over the place."

Mackie continued: "At one point, he allegedly entered the women's washroom and ripped off a stall door. At another party, he 'thought everyone should go home' and so threw a TV off the counter facefirst. And every time he saw a certain ultra-hyper MuchMusic VJ, he screamed, 'You got some dope?' at the top of his lungs."

With a feline friend, 1990. (Denise Howard / Material republished with the express permission of: Vancouver Sun, a division of Postmedia Network Inc.)

However, the memory Art left with many was a comment he made about the year's big winner, Alannah Myles, who, after years of slogging it out in Toronto as a singer and actress, had scored an international hit with "Black Velvet," which subsequently earned Junos for single of the year, album of the year, and most promising female vocalist. When her name came up, Art didn't hesitate to speak dismissively of her—something he later regretted—although he viewed her success as emblematic of the Canadian music industry's unfathomable praise of mediocrity.

> They're wimps, the whole Canadian music industry is a pile of wussies. It sounds like one big fucking beer ad—it's disgusting. And all these heavy metal bands with their cynical ploy for radio play with their ballads—come on. They call me cynical?

Two weeks after the Junos, Art and the Showdogs were opening for the Tragically Hip at the Concert Hall in Toronto. With a video for "Bound for Vegas" in rotation on Much-Music that combined live performance with subtle jabs at a wide range of celebrities, the pairing of Art with the Hip should have been a triumphant snapshot of the current state of

Canadian rock. But even then, Art's bullshit detector was fully engaged, as he responded to the soon-to-be familiar chant of "Hip! Hip! Hip!" during his set with caustic remarks like "Your heroes will be on soon."

Things went more smoothly when the Showdogs and the Pursuit of Happiness hit the road together in June, as Art and Moe Berg seemed to complement each other more naturally as songwriters. TPOH also included guitarist Kris Abbott and backing vocalist Leslie Stanwyck, who provided some gender balance, much as Susann Richter did in the Showdogs.

The quest for new ears hit a peak on June 26, when Feldman added Art to a bill with Australia's Midnight Oil at UBC's Thunderbird Stadium. Facing a crowd of twenty-six thousand, by far his biggest since the Young Canadians' tour with the Boomtown Rats, Art and the Showdogs rose to the challenge while giving some of his long-time hometown supporters a glimpse of what was still possible in terms of mass acceptance.

Showdogs, 1990. (James O'Mara)

Critics in Canada were certainly doing their part by showering *Sexual Roulette* with praise and getting readers up to speed on Art's punk rock credentials. It all seemed to dovetail perfectly with an offer he received soon after that he couldn't turn down. Toronto filmmaker Bruce McDonald had originally wanted to cast Iggy Pop in the role of a wealthy, eccentric rock star for his second feature, *Highway 61*. It was the follow-up to McDonald's indie breakthrough, *Roadkill*, based in part on the true story of Toronto post-punk band A Neon Rome, who had been sent on a disastrous tour of small northern Ontario towns, and whose lead singer, Neal Arbic, had taken a vow of silence that ultimately marked the band's end. With a larger budget, McDonald retained most of the cast and crew of *Roadkill* for *Highway 61*, the story of a hapless barber from Thunder Bay played by Don McKellar who, upon discovering a corpse one day outside his shop, is convinced by a visiting band roadie played by Valerie Buhagiar that the body is her brother's and they must return it to New Orleans for burial. The woman's actual intention is to smuggle drugs across the border in the coffin, the twist being that throughout the journey a man claiming to be Satan pursues the pair in an effort to consummate the deal he's made for the dead man's soul.

As McDonald explained to *Take One* magazine in 2004, "we had Telefilm Canada, Channel 4 in England, and some German money. That was very encouraging. The British bought the film on the strength of *Roadkill*, which was great. We also had sold them on Iggy Pop being in the movie, but he pulled out at the last minute. [Producer] Colin [Brunton] was working on him, and he had verbally agreed, but that year, at Cannes, he was appearing in a John Waters film and I think it went to his head. Now he thought he was a movie star and he no longer wanted to be in this low-budget Canadian movie. It was very weird. It was a few weeks before production was to start, and he pulled out. We were feeling very bad because we had sold the movie on Iggy being in it. He was to play the character that Art Bergmann plays. But we went ahead anyway, and there is a little dog in the beginning of the film that we called Iggy Pup. We were all big Iggy fans, but not anymore."

Despite his lack of acting experience, Art gave a great, over-the-top performance as Otto, who occupies a Memphis mansion with fellow reclusive musician Margo, played by Tracy Wright. In one of the film's most memorable scenes, the pair releases chickens inside the mansion and hunts them with guns for that night's dinner, all while Tom Jones's "It's Not Unusual" blasts on the stereo.

With *Highway 61* scheduled for release in September 1991, it was poised to become another milestone in Art's ongoing struggle to transition from cult hero to household name. But getting there still required a radical overhaul of his lifestyle, with the first step being the dissolution of the Showdogs. "It reached a point where Susann just couldn't deal with Art and me anymore," Ray Fulber recalled. "Everything was revolving around the drug-taking and both of us had to clean up. For me, it was an easy choice because I didn't want to lose Susann, but I imagine it was harder for Art because he was losing what I like to believe was the best band he ever had. I don't think he even had a steady band after that."

> What really happened with the Showdogs was that I left the band because I did not feel they were up to the task of my newer work. I told them one evening that we seemed to get shittier every time we rehearsed my new songs. That was it, it all ended that one night, and the next day I started working on demos for the next album. It was a chickenshit thing to do.

Whether breaking up the Showdogs was necessary or not, it would mark the beginning of an entirely new phase of Art's life, one guided by the person who would truly keep him alive.

A CRYPTIC CLUE
WITHOUT A CROSSWORD

IN MARCH 1991, the Juno Awards were handed out at the Queen Elizabeth Theatre in Vancouver, the first time the gala had been held somewhere other than Toronto. Yet, despite the hometown advantage and the universal critical praise doled out for *Sexual Roulette*, Art received no nominations. Furthermore, he and virtually every other figure from the Vancouver underground were nowhere to be seen, except at an unsanctioned post-ceremony blowout at the Smash Gallery, where Randy Bachman dropped by and played a raunchy version of the Guess Who's "American Woman," with the Subhumans' Brian Goble mercilessly trampling all over Burton Cummings' original take.

Art's snub underscored the reality that Duke Street still wielded little power in the Canadian music industry, and the only remedy to that was for Art to somehow finally make a jump to the majors. From Sam Feldman's position, the clearest path to achieving this was to approach PolyGram Records, also under the umbrella of Duke Street's distributor, MCA. Since the mid-1970s, the Dutch/German–based PolyGram had been making significant moves into the North American market, acquiring labels including Island and A&M, and establishing a Canadian branch office in Montreal. This operation moved to Toronto in 1990, whereupon PolyGram's Canadian vice-president of A&R, Montreal-born Corky Laing—the former drummer for heavy metal pioneers Mountain—began scouting new talent to boost the label's domestic catalogue. Given his track record, Art seemed, if not a safe bet, then at least a prestigious signing for Laing, once he became familiar with Art's body of work.

"As an A&R department, it was definitely our focus to sign Canadian artists," Laing said. "I had a lot of friends in New York who would call me up looking for a deal, but I had to turn them down because this was what we had decided to do. Funnily enough, the first artist I pitched to [PolyGram Canada president] Peter Erdmann was Alanis Morissette. My brother lived in Ottawa, where she was from, and somehow got a tape to me, and it was a dance record. I took it to Peter and said, 'Look, she's young but she's obviously very talented and has a great attitude,' and Peter just flatly said, 'We're not signing any dance artists.' So that was a big fish that got away."

Although Laing acknowledged that there was no shortage of Canadian artists doing interesting things, one of his problems was that too many others he encountered were making music that clearly imitated popular acts from elsewhere in the world. He didn't get that impression the moment he heard Art. "What immediately appealed to me about Art was not only his originality, but his I-don't-give-a-fuck attitude. He came across as a human being, not someone trying to be a celebrity, and I really respected that."

> **Interview with the *Vancouver Sun*, June 8, 1991:**
> **[Sam Feldman] did all the talking. I didn't have to do a thing. It feels pretty good, but it's kinda late, isn't it guys?**

The timing was in fact right for the move, as Art had amassed enough material over the previous year to form a solid foundation for a new album. Not having the Showdogs involved presented a challenge, but Art's frame of mind was the best it had been in some time, largely because of his new relationship with Sherri Decembrini. She was a decade younger than Art, but had already lived—and rejected—the life that was expected of her. She'd been born in New Westminster, BC, and at ten days old had been adopted by the family of Donald Watt, a Canadian navy veteran, insurance adjuster, and auxiliary RCMP officer who settled his brood in Trail, after five years of living in Vancouver. Blond and strikingly beautiful, at age sixteen Sherri married a local boy named Scott Decembrini, who had steady employment with a construction equipment supply company. They had a daughter, Naomi, a year later, in 1980, but in short order Sherri was longing for the life most women her age got to experience. "I'd quit school when I got married, so my education became reading every book I'd heard mentioned on CBC Radio," she said. "I actually learned a lot for being stranded in the middle of nowhere." When she was twenty, a counsellor convinced her to train to become a nurse's aide, a job she quickly found she wasn't suited to do. "I couldn't believe how mean all the nurses were to the patients. It was all just about getting them clean and fed and sticking them in front of the TV. I couldn't handle that."

By 1985, Sherri had determined to split from her husband and live her own life. She took some university courses in anthropology, leading to a job running a small museum in Trail, but it was a course she took in basic journalism that fully captured her imagination. As she grew more confident in her writing abilities, she was increasingly attracted to pursuing opportunities in Vancouver. On one trip to the city, she took a chance in contacting *Nite Moves*, an upstart monthly magazine that for a few years provided some competition for the *Georgia Straight*'s weekly coverage of the city's cultural scene. At first, the publisher assigned her to sell ads, but when that turned out to be a non-starter, she began contributing regular reviews and eventually proved capable enough to take over as editor when the position became open.

The job immediately connected Sherri to the major players in the Vancouver music industry, who sought her influence by wining and dining her at every opportunity. And with a new boyfriend who earned a sizable income, money wasn't a concern, though they had frequent spats over their musical tastes, fuelled by Sherri's growing disgust with the vapid musicians she was forced to cover. However, she didn't truly comprehend how vapid they were until the moment she finally crossed paths with Art, in May 1990. "It was at a press conference to announce the

Junos coming to Vancouver," she recalled. "We were all there mostly for the free drinks, and he was at a table with some other people I knew. But as soon as we started talking, it felt like we were the only two people in the room. We were the last to leave and ended up at the Town Pump, necking like we thought we were invisible. I actually didn't know anything about Art, apart from seeing a bit of the 'Our Little Secret' video. I had a writer, Greg Potter, who covered local music, and he knew all those guys, which left me to be able to focus on writing about more high-profile stuff. But after that initial meeting, I made an effort to listen to all his music."

With Art still touring in support of *Sexual Roulette*, neither attempted to pursue things further until a few weeks later—on July 12, to be precise—when Art obtained Sherri's phone number from Potter and asked her bluntly if she would like to have an affair. Sherri's response? "I said, 'Yeah, I'll meet you at 86 Street Music Hall in an hour. July 13 is my birthday, and in those twenty-four hours I got a crash course in who Art was. A month later, he gave me a ring with an inscription on it: 'Art & Sherri, Summer 1990.' I was like, 'This is only for the summer?'" It wouldn't be, as Art possessed qualities no man in Sherri's life had ever displayed—he was honest, outspoken, and endlessly creative, and exuded a generous spirit. Above all, he viewed Sherri as a complete person. Still, it wasn't enough to convince some of her friends that pledging herself to Art was a wise decision. "The man I'd been with was really wealthy. He didn't have to work—he just played golf every day, owned Lamborghinis, the whole bit. So a lot of people told me it would be a big mistake to leave him. But Art and I just clicked. We had the same sort of religious upbringing, we liked the same music, we read the same books—we talked about running away and getting married that very day, but of course everything is more complicated than that."

By then, Sherri knew her biological parents' identities, having learned that her name at birth was Ivers. She'd placed a notice in the *Vancouver Sun* asking either of them to get in touch, and had received a surprisingly prompt reply from her mother, who was living in Kelowna. "She came up to visit, this tiny little lady who had a drinking problem, among other things. The first thing she said was, 'My God, do you look like your dad,' and from that moment I became consumed by finding out who I actually was." A series of phone calls to previously unknown relatives led Sherri to an aunt who gave her the news that her father, Jack Ivers, was in prison, a place he'd spent a considerable portion of his life for drug and burglary offences. "When I was born, he'd just gotten seven years for bringing heroin over the border," Sherri said. "But he was a really smart guy. He was an electrician, although he used those skills a lot to rewire grow houses and make meters run backwards. Then he learned to be a locksmith in jail and could make keys for anything. I adored him, mainly because he was the opposite of my adopted father, but also because he justified why I thought about things differently than other people. At the same time, I came to realize through meeting my parents that I'd basically been born an addict."

Sherri continued to grow close to her birth mother as well, and after she and Art had both broken things off with their respective partners, Sherri found an apartment in downtown Vancouver where she, her daughter, her mother, and Art all lived for the remainder of 1990. Sherri continued to work at the magazine during the day, and at night she and Art would most often go to shows, leaving Naomi in the care of Sherri's mother. It proved to be a creatively stimulating time for Art, and when he played some of the new songs he'd been writing to Greg Potter, the writer told his boss that he thought Art had written some of them about her. Sherri replied that they were all about her; Art just didn't know it yet.

As might have been expected, Art couldn't keep his self-doubt completely in check, despite the positive turn his life had taken. Even what may have been his first bona fide love song, "Faithlessly Yours," contained sentiments stemming from the inherent risks that came with jumping into a committed relationship after previous failed attempts. It also made a none-too-subtle reference to Sherri's career: "God placed an ad in her paper / A cryptic clue without a crossword / How could I have known she worked that paper / The sweetest sound the world has heard."

Art's reckoning with his past behaviour reared its head on "If She Could Sing," summed up in the lines "When she finds her voice I'll listen / For a clue to what was missing / When I placed the emphasis on mine." This was new psychological territory for Art, though it was never in the cards for him to write a completely relationship-based album, given the state of the world at that moment. The Soviet Union had crumbled, and a form of freedom his father had briefly known in childhood had returned to the former Eastern Bloc nations, albeit with strings attached. Art processed this on "American Wife" by shining a light on capitalism's seductive attributes. "Watch the reunited Germans / You know they make the best businessmen / But we've got a billion hamburgers, free Coke / White collar criminals and money for dope."

There was also the raging conflict in the Persian Gulf to contend with, and like most Canadians, Art struggled to make sense of it while watching the destruction unfold in real time. But no matter what the US government fed reporters on a daily basis, its underlying motivation was clear. Along with "American Wife," "Baby Needs Oil" provided a jagged counterbalance to the hummable love songs, while attempting to look at the situation objectively. "I've uncovered an unearthly delight / TV battles in my desert night / A Superbowl of candy missiles in flight / Tell me why are all the newsmen white / My baby needs oil / She's been drinking like it's going out of style / My baby's love's on the boil / She's found a new land to soil."

In light of geopolitical realities, Art resurrected the Poisoned-era track "God's Little Gift," co-written with Bill Scherk, to emphasize his disgust with countries imposing their will on other territories, but that frustration ultimately reached a dead end on "I Can't Change This World," another semi-spoken-word piece, crafted almost like a diary entry with the date January 15, 1991, anchoring it to a time and place. Art walks the streets of Vancouver's Japantown, on his way to meet Sherri. His thoughts are consumed by what he's been seeing on the news, such as a correspondent talking about the thrill of being missed by enemy fire. Art's response in the song? "Me, I'm supposed to be writing a hit." It leads to darker musings on how humans have the capacity to hate one another for the strangest of reasons, which sets him off into a spiral of self-loathing. "Sit around all day just waiting for something clever to say / I'm losing my grip on this pen and feel like searching for my syringe again / Makes me hate my own song."

Yet Art's belief in rock and roll carried him through the writing of two other songs that would serve as pillars for the new album. "Remember Her Name" was a brooding, mid-tempo rocker that painted a bleak portrait of a Manhattan prostitute who, when seen from one angle, embodied the tragic essence of British singer Marianne Faithfull, and when viewed from another perspective could actually have been Faithfull herself after falling from her lofty perch as Mick Jagger's 1960s girlfriend, succumbing to heroin addiction, and living on the streets of London until her career rebounded with the 1979 album *Broken English*. Art heard his own story in a lot of Faithfull's damaged poetry, and replicating it placed many of his new songs in the netherworld occupied by more and more formerly cutting-edge artists now grappling with the ravages of time and misguided decisions, producing music steeped in new technology that nonetheless reflected their own fading grandeur.

Still, the sense of rejuvenation Sherri had infused into his life brought Art back from that precipice, as did the inspiration he took from a songwriter six years his junior who embodied the same "fuck it" attitude that had always fuelled Art's best work. Paul Westerberg had led the Replacements from hometown-hero status in their native Minneapolis to having international music media outlets deem them rock and roll's last hope at the end of the 1980s. All four members were unabashedly excessive drinkers who revelled in self-sabotage—their infamous 1986 *Saturday Night Live* appearance being the prime example—but throughout it all Westerberg amassed a body of work that was by turns hilarious and heart-wrenching, rooted in equal measure in a disdain for societal norms and a genuine gift for expressing it through contrarian language. Coincidentally, Westerberg had also written a song called "I Hate Music" two years after the Young Canadians' track was released on *Vancouver Complication*. If that had been a sign to Art that they were kindred spirits, he didn't fully let on until he was moved to write "Message from Paul," just as it appeared the Replacements were on the verge of a mainstream breakthrough. It had been building since the band's 1987 album *Pleased To Meet Me*, which became a touchstone for the production aesthetic of *Sexual Roulette*. However, instead of turning "Message from Paul" into a straight fan letter, Art crafted it into a hallucinatory, pseudo-psychedelic track, equating it to his own "road to Damascus" moment, like the one described in the Bible when the apostle Paul is converted after encountering Jesus in the form of a divine light. It was the sort of metaphor that Westerberg would have never dared to attempt, yet Art turned it into the perfect tribute with the simple summation that "It could mean nothing at all."

In the end, Art saved the most revealing moments for "Ruin My Life," a moving acknowledgement of Sherri's devotion, which had arrived at a time when Art needed it the most. She'd known about Art's addiction from the time they'd met, and in some ways this strengthened their bond. Art, knowing full well the value of being with a person who intimately understood that struggle, channelled those sentiments into a song that, with patented dark humour, attempted to say goodbye to his former life. "Take my drugs and throw 'em out the window / Change my bed, change my head / Everything was going wrong until now / Take every promise I've ever broken / Turn them into a vow."

Corky Laing recalled, "Art and Sherri were basically inseparable when I got to know them. She was there for everything, and that admittedly got me a little nervous, because I'd experienced that in Mountain with Felix Pappalardi and his wife, Gail, which later ended in tragic circumstances. But looking back, it's easy to see the positive effect she had on him."

By the start of April 1991, Art was ready to record again. Given everyone's satisfaction with *Sexual Roulette*, full faith was placed in Chris Wardman to again handle production duties. And without the Showdogs, Wardman had the added task of assembling a band suited to the material. Wardman's contacts were in Toronto, so it was agreed to have Art fly in and hold sessions at Manta Sound, where any memories of John Cale's keyboard obsession would finally be banished. To do this, Wardman decided to keep things simple, adding guitar parts himself whenever it seemed appropriate to embellish Art's own instrumental tracks, and enlisting his former Blue Peter bandmate Jason Sniderman—son of Canadian music-retail king Sam "the Record Man" Sniderman—on keyboards. Accompanying Art from Vancouver was bassist Jamey Koch, an associate of Bob Rock's who also occasionally played in one of Chris Houston's projects, the Strolling Clones. Getting the call to play drums was Toronto's Joel Anderson, whom Wardman trusted after his work with Neo A4.

"I'd gone to Vancouver to see where things were at and I found that Art had been working with Jamey on arranging the new songs, so they were prepared when they got to Toronto," Wardman said. "I think the drummer they wanted to use couldn't make the trip for some reason, so I brought in Joel, who was kind of my go-to guy when I needed someone in a pinch. The same went for Jason when it came to keyboards; he was someone I could always rely on. It ended up being a pretty good band. I was able to get my friends in Breeding Ground to lend us their rehearsal space and we got the songs fairly tight before going into the studio. I don't recall a lot of time being wasted.

"The fact that some of the songs had more of a pop-friendly sound wasn't intentional. It was just the direction in which they naturally seemed to want to go. Corky Laing would drop by the studio occasionally to check in on us, but he would mostly just hang out and tell war stories. He was great to be around. We were basically allowed to do whatever we wanted."

> I don't know what a hit single is. I don't write hit singles. Each song to me is more important than anything else I've ever done. As far as I'm concerned, *Sexual Roulette* is radio friendly. Most of the songs I keep playing I hope are still apropos today. The '80s to me was one amorphous mess. I can't tell one event from the next, or one defining moment. Music to me is like the Sex Pistols' early stuff when they didn't know what they were doing but they were playing rock and roll. It was defined, then the Pistols came out and redefined it. Until Nirvana, I don't think it got redefined again.

Jamey Koch was part of the first generation of Vancouver teens to be drawn into the local punk scene and was a fan of Art's for many years before getting to know him in the late 1980s, when they both lived in the same neighbourhood off Commercial Drive. As a bassist, he'd cultivated a reputation for being able to insert himself into a wide range of musical situations, which prompted Art to contact him for assistance in fleshing out the new songs. "I was excited to work that closely with Art, and we made demos for songs like 'American Wife' and 'Message from Paul' in some little studios over the period of a few weeks," Koch said. "What I

Art and Sherri. (ALEX WATERHOUSE-HAYWARD)

remember most is that we did a lot of singing together, which I think was new for him. But our harmonies sounded great, and I really enjoyed that part of it. We could tell right away that what we were doing was good."

That feeling carried over into the Toronto sessions, which according to Koch went smoothly over the course of another couple of weeks, with the musicians forging an instant rapport. Wardman cultivated this atmosphere by installing a sign at the mixing desk that read "This IS the mix," emphasizing that his aim was to capture the songs as they were played, with minimal overdubbing. That approach seemed to suit Art fine, and Koch said there were never any confrontational moments. "Art was always focused on getting the best results possible, and as long as everyone was in agreement on that, there were never any problems. From my perspective, I've always thought that the image some people might have of him being 'difficult' isn't accurate, or at least overblown by the media. He's just a great all-around musician, and I think everyone who's ever worked with him knows and respects that."

With the new album in the can and the ink on his new contract with PolyGram dry by summer 1991, Art was well positioned once again to take a run at mainstream acceptance. He'd even agreed to simply call the album *Art Bergmann*, after being convinced that its working title, *The Moist, Dark Thing Is Beautiful*, wouldn't do much to boost sales. Its two most upbeat tracks, "Faithlessly Yours" and "If She Could Sing," were earmarked as initial singles, with "Message from Paul" standing by as a third. However, when the subject of videos came up, it was decided to take a completely unorthodox approach. Art proposed using the label's allotted video budget to book a trip to Spain—a nod to his interest in the Spanish Civil War— where he, Sherri, Laing, and video director Roy Pike could shoot raw footage that would be the basis for three potential clips.

"It was a really renegade move," Laing said of the Spanish sojourn. "The way things worked then was you paid $20,000 for a day of shooting on a set in Toronto. So we said, 'Fuck it, let's take that money and go somewhere and have a good time.' As soon as we arrived in Madrid, we went looking for a place to rent a car in order to drive around the southern part of the country. We found a garage where we could rent a convertible Ferrari for $1,000 US, but they also had a beautiful convertible Buick Skylark that cost $5,000 to rent because it was American-made. So we went with the Skylark and spent the next several days on the road. Roy would be hanging off the trunk, trying to get different angles, and we'd shoot at any interesting place we stumbled upon, which included a lot of cafés."

Pike said the decision to go to Spain dated back to when he had been approached to make a video for "Bound for Vegas," and his instinctive response was to avoid the obvious. "When the label and management started talking about going to Vegas to shoot the video, that was the last place I wanted to go. I'd been to Spain a lot and loved it, so I said, 'Let's go to Barcelona. It won't make any sense, but it'll be cool as hell.' Art was into it, but Sam Feldman hated the idea, and he basically had the final word. But the seed was planted."

Pike added that he'd probably pitched Spain unsuccessfully to every client he had at that time, but when the opportunity came around again to pitch it to Laing, it was immediately accepted. "Corky hated the process of making videos in those days, mainly the cost. He also hated the word *should*. There seemed to be this orthodoxy in the Canadian music business that things had to be done in certain ways. Whenever I was with Corky and someone said to him, 'You should do this,' he turned right off. At one point he said to me, 'Why can't we just get some plane tickets and go somewhere cool to make it?' And my response was basically, 'Yeah, why can't we?' I was confident that I had the technical ability to pull it off by myself. The only problem in doing that was we were putting ourselves in a situation where we had no control. Remember, this was long before cellphones."

The other problem, Laing and Pike soon discovered, was Art's physical state. According to Pike, despite Sherri's support, Art was still in the grip of a heroin habit, which was evident as the trip got under way. "Right after Art signed the PolyGram deal in Toronto and Corky called me to do the videos, I remember a bunch of us going out for drinks to celebrate. It was a great night, everyone was really happy for Art, but then he went back to Vancouver, and I'm not sure what happened. The next time I saw him, when he got off the plane in Spain, that guy looked like fucking death. I was like, 'Holy shit, we're in trouble here.' I was innocent to all that stuff, and I learned he was in withdrawal. One of the first shoots we did was at the aqueduct in Toledo, and Art was so tired he could barely walk."

It became a moment when Laing's experience in the rock and roll trenches of the 1970s proved most valuable, as he recognized what needed to happen. "Corky didn't say anything, he just did what he had to do to get Art what he needed—in this city, Madrid, that he'd never been to before, mind you," Pike said. "When he made a connection, he told me to go to this café and give money to this guy, who then pulled a big aluminum-foil ball out of his mouth. When I brought it to Corky, he started unwrapping it, peeling off layer after layer until it was clear there was nothing inside. So Corky, being who he is, goes to this guy's house in a barrio and starts yelling from the street, 'You son of a bitch! You burned the wrong person, motherfucker! I'm gonna come up there with an axe and chop you to pieces!' And so he got the drugs."

When it came to addressing obstacles of the legal variety, Laing had arranged through PolyGram Spain to hire a local fixer named Antonio, who doubled as a production assistant and accompanied them in his own van. His presence became necessary when it was discovered that outside of the large cities, Spain was a much more conservative society than anyone had anticipated. "We'd decided that Sherri would drive the Skylark, and when the guy we rented it from realized that, he started shitting his pants, because even something like a woman driving a car that fancy was frowned upon," Pike recalled. "I think, in general, everyone we encountered on that trip was pretty disgusted by us. I was a grunge kid, and of course Art had his issues with authority, so wherever we went, people didn't hide what they thought of us. For one shoot, we wanted to get some romantic footage of Art and Sherri at an old church. We found one, and I started filming them banging on the front doors. As they were doing that, a guy drove up and started screaming at us for disrespecting the church. So Antonio starts yelling back, telling this guy to lighten up, we're only making a movie. I got some of that on film and we thought it would be hilarious to put it at the beginning of 'Faithlessly Yours.'"

Aside from the occasional confrontation, the rest of the week went relatively smoothly, with Pike relying on his rented Arriflex 16mm camera and a variety of film for different lighting situations. When shooting lip-synched parts, Art sang along to a ghetto blaster, and the overall mercenary approach led Pike to improvise. "There's something I've always wanted to take credit for," he said. "For a standard video shoot, there would be a sound guy with a cumbersome and expensive Nagra machine to synch up the music. When CDs came out, they were time-coded, just like VHS tapes were. So I thought, 'If we use VHS with a monitor, we can synch that up with a CD and it won't cost anything.' That's all we needed for what we were doing."

There was a collective sigh of relief at the end of the week when everyone felt satisfied that there was enough usable footage, yet the pressure caused Laing to come down with a painful case of shingles. Meanwhile, Pike had his own problem to deal with after losing his passport on the beach at Alicante, which forced him to remain an extra week after everyone had gone home. "I had to stay with Antonio in Madrid, and the first thing he did was take me out to buy new clothes, which was a not-so-subtle way of saying he didn't want to be seen in public with me the way I dressed. So, when I look back on that whole trip, I remember it as being equal parts fun and stress."

For his part, Laing remembers the trip as a success. "It was really a fun time, and I'm proud of how those videos captured Art's true, rough-around-the-edges personality," he said. "I remember once Denise Donlon, who was running MuchMusic, asked me, 'How were you able to make all these videos in exotic locations?' When I explained it to her, she couldn't believe it. Nobody had ever done anything like that before."

Art and Sherri ultimately tied the knot in Vancouver on August 22, 1991, just over a year after they first met. "Corky had kind of fake-married us at the Sagrada Família in Barcelona, but I'm actually not sure why we did it at that moment when we got back," Sherri said, bemusedly. "I guess Art had received a big cheque from the record company, so maybe that was enough reason. I bought a second-hand wedding dress, and the people we invited showed up either dressed to the nines or in shorts. The whole thing cost $200. It was so weird. That was the first time I'd ever met Art's family, but they were so nice. They instantly became my family."

Art Bergmann was released in September 1991—preceded by "Faithlessly Yours," which managed to climb as high as No. 11 on *RPM* magazine's Canadian singles chart. Although PolyGram pulled out all the stops in terms of promotion, in hindsight it's clear that the album arrived in the midst of what was one of the most significant months in recent pop and rock history. Across North America, kids who the previous month had flocked to record stores to buy Metallica's (Bob Rock–produced) self-titled album now salivated over getting their hands on Guns N' Roses' magnum opus *Use Your Illusion I* and *II*. Others snatched up the Red Hot Chili Peppers' *Blood Sugar Sex Magik* and later came back in droves for Nirvana's *Nevermind* and Pearl Jam's *Ten*, the latter released with little initial fanfare in late August. Earlier that summer, the first Lollapalooza tour had launched, headlined by founder Perry Farrell's band Jane's Addiction and featuring Nine Inch Nails, along with the Butthole Surfers and rapper Ice-T's heavy-metal project Body Count.

There was no denying that a musical revolution was under way as figures who had helped establish the North American underground music community now rose to positions of power in the media and at major labels. Without US and European label partners, Art was left in the uncomfortable position of trying to be heard amid the seemingly endless stream of soon-to-be classic records flowing into shops on a weekly basis, while simultaneously confirming his rightful position within Canada's new "alternative rock" hierarchy. Nobody foresaw this, least of all his label. "For all of us at PolyGram, Art was golden," Laing said. "And for me, he was an international artist who transcended all trends. He was Canada's Lou Reed, as far as I was concerned, and didn't need any more of a promotional push than that."

The biggest barrier between Art and his potential audience remained touring, something made much more difficult now in the absence of a regular band. A proposed cross-Canada tour at the end of 1991 was unceremoniously scrapped when Sam Feldman and Jeff Rogers—for reasons neither is sure about—severed ties with Art, leaving him at the mercy of outside forces that presented him with an offer he could not refuse.

CHAPTER
10

A BUTTERFLY
IN DRYING CONCRETE

THE FOUNDATIONS OF POLYGRAM RECORDS CANADA had become increasingly unstable by 1992, as its parent corporation continued to diversify and swallow up other labels around the world. It was a time when nearly every major North American record company was ceding power to large conglomerates aiming to bring previously disconnected entertainment industries together under a single umbrella, all for the benefit of their shareholders. Sony had taken control of the venerable labels CBS and EMI at the same time that it had acquired Columbia Pictures, and its archrival, the Matsushita Group (a.k.a. Panasonic), countered by purchasing MCA's music and film divisions, which later became Universal Music and Universal Pictures.

In July 1992, the *New York Times* praised PolyGram's similar investments in Hollywood and Broadway, while noting that its takeovers of A&M Records and Island Records, along with the success of artists on the PolyGram label itself, had boosted the company's overall share of the US record market to 12.5 per cent. Specifically, the article cited PolyGram's discovery of a singer named Billy Ray Cyrus, whose debut single, "Achy Breaky Heart," infected the collective consciousness like an incurable rash that year. "The unknown country music singer was signed to a PolyGram multi-record contract roughly three years ago," business reporter Geraldine Fabrikant explained to her non-musically educated readers. "Such contracts are generally for several hundred thousand dollars. His record made the country charts and later the pop charts. Such a crossover ultimately introduces the singer to a broader audience and increases record sales. Undoubtedly, Mr. Cyrus's contract will be renegotiated, but the profit potential for PolyGram, if the singer's success continues, is likely to be significantly greater than it might have been for a higher-cost performer."

Crossover, profit potential, higher-cost performer—such terminology had always been a part of the music business, but never before had these notions been the sole motivating factor for record company decisions. No one could make a rational argument that "Achy Breaky Heart" contained any artistic merit, apart from possessing the same basic appeal as "Happy Birthday" or "Row Row Row Your Boat," and that was essentially the point. Music was becoming a commodity just like any other natural resource, with its value determined by current earnings and projected future sales. In the grand scheme, it meant that PolyGram Canada was merely a decorative accessory within the corporate machine, one of those assets that could easily be redirected to another division without any serious ramifications. That's precisely what happened in spring 1992, when PolyGram Canada was rebranded PolyGram Group Canada, putting an end to Corky Laing's plans of growing a roster of homegrown talent. From then on, the Toronto office would concentrate on back catalogue releases and cheaply produced albums for the classical music market that required little promotion.

Once again, a record company had left Art twisting in the wind. In the absence of a band with whom he could play steady gigs, 1992 was shaping up to be a lost year until he was tossed a lifeline in the form of one of the many multi-artist excursions conceived in the wake of Lollapalooza's success. Organizers MCA Concerts dubbed it the "Big, Bad & Groovy Tour," although, as it was Canada's first attempt at something of this sort, many naturally chose to call it "Hoser-palooza." It was definitely on a smaller scale, with dates booked mainly at university venues across the country to coincide with the start of the school year. Topping the bill was Bootsauce, a Montreal funk-rock outfit that did little to hide the debt it owed to the Red Hot Chili Peppers, and was coincidentally another of Laing's signings to PolyGram. The tour took its name from a song on the group's new sophomore album, *Bull*, the last notable domestic PolyGram release. Joining them, and reinforcing the Lollapalooza aesthetic, was Vancouver's Pure, whose 1992 debut album, produced by Jerry Harrison of Talking Heads, offered a Canadian take on the Britpop movement that was providing a counterbalance to American grunge. Only their fellow Vancouverites Sons of Freedom presented themselves as something approaching originality. Having established a punishing sound that flirted with post-punk and hard rock in equal measure, they'd landed a deal with LA-based Slash Records for their outstanding 1988 self-titled debut album. The band was eventually picked up by MCA Records Canada, releasing *Gump* in 1991, which unfortunately would be their last collection of original material.

Where Art fit into all of that was anybody's guess. He was forced to play solo sets with an electric guitar, and his disdain for the entire enterprise manifested itself right from the tour's opening in Vancouver, which quickly made him a pariah among his tourmates. It had been generally accepted that he would travel on the bus rented for Bootsauce and their crew, but neither they nor Art wanted anything to do with each other.

> It was pretty nasty. I was butt-boy—blame it on Art. Anything that went wrong, it must be Art. Bootsauce had way too many managers, and I had Greyhound tickets to get from gig to gig because no one would allow me on the buses. I would supposedly be a bad influence. These were adults who drank far more than I could ever hope to drink because I don't like to drink a lot of beer. I like rocket fuel, that's my weakness.

"I should have been with him on that tour," Sherri said. "It was such a shitty thing that they did to him, and it really pissed me off because Art is truly a wonderful human being. But they saw him as a drunken junkie who would do anything. He had quit by then—sort of—so he wasn't sick, but he was constantly trying to catch up with everybody else on the road. It was a logistical nightmare."

As the tour rambled across the Prairies, Art fell into a routine of dragging himself and his guitar to the local Greyhound depot at 6 a.m. to get to the next city in time for that night's show. In Regina, he got off schedule after being kicked off the bus for an open bottle of wine and had to resort to hitchhiking. It led to an unexpected scene when Toronto band the Lowest of the Low passed him on their way into town for a gig. Seeing one of his favourite songwriters reduced to such a level was something the Low's frontman, Ron Hawkins, would never forget. "We were on the other side of the highway, and as we blew by him I just caught a glimpse and was like, 'Hey, that's Art Bergmann,'" he said. "The other guys didn't believe me, and it wasn't until about a week later that we found out what was going on with Art on that tour. It really set me off thinking about how ridiculous it was that the guy who I considered the godfather of Canadian punk rock was hitchhiking at this point in his career. Here was someone who's given so much to the Canadian music industry, and this was how it treated him, kicking him down the highway."

Hawkins had become a fan of Art's after hearing *Crawl with Me*, and in the year before forming the Lowest of the Low in 1991, he would play songs from *Sexual Roulette* while trying to earn a living busking in downtown Toronto. That moment on the Trans-Canada Highway planted the seed for the song "Life Imitates Art," which would appear on the Low's 1994 sophomore album *Hallucigenia*: "We all felt pretty stunned, watching him hitch out on Highway One / A guitar against his elbow, knowing more than they'll ever know…The twisted punch-line says they'll understand you when you're dead / You say that you're not angry, just 'savagely disappointed' / I just want you to know, when you feel like letting go / There're a thousand souls like me taking shelter in your coat."

When the Big, Bad & Groovy Tour mercifully concluded at the end of September, it did indeed feel as if outside forces were conspiring to make Art disappear, literally in at least one instance. After such a soul-destroying experience, it seemed only natural to turn back to drugs as a remedy. When signs of that became evident to some of Sherri's friends and family, they reignited arguments that Art would drag them both down to the depths of depravity. From all this came a situation that might have been tailor-made for an episode of American daytime trash TV. "My birth father's sister, even though she didn't drink or do drugs, was completely fucked," Sherri explained. "She used to date guys from the Clark Park Gang and had other men in her life die under mysterious circumstances. She had her own marijuana grow operation too, so there was always a level of paranoia within her. My sister wanted to get in on that business and for some reason started telling my aunt all these negative things about Art, about how he had ruined my life. So my aunt responded by saying she'd hired a hit man to kill him."

Sherri's birth father—out of prison at that point—took the threat seriously and advised Sherri not to allow Art to leave their apartment. When she told him that was impossible, he did what he thought was within his means to protect them. "The door to our apartment was partially broken because I'd kicked it in one day when I'd forgotten my keys," Sherri said. "So one day my dad called a carpenter and they put a bulletproof door in. Steel grey. Every other apartment door in that building was wood, and now here we were with a metal door. My neighbours thought it was pretty funny, because I don't think they knew the reason behind it. I wouldn't have told them. But that was the last time I talked to my sister. I still don't understand how she could have said those things about Art that were so wrong."

The threat to his life merely reinforced the lesson Art had learned from the Big, Bad & Groovy Tour, that no one in the music industry was prepared to take him seriously anymore unless he got his shit together. As 1993 dawned, Art faced the grim reality of kicking his heroin habit cold-turkey, and once he was over the roughest parts of that, he was able to focus on songwriting again.

Overshadowing it all was the death of his father, Frank, on January 10. The old man had endured nearly eighty years by following the righteous path and leaving an enduring legacy of honest, hard work and community building. If there was any way to pay tribute to this, Art at the very least could rally his creative energy and take one more stab at this crazy trade he had chosen—or, more accurately, had chosen him.

One of the first songs to come out fully formed was "Beatles in Hollywood." It was another piece first conceived as a poem, and it set an ominous tone by vividly portraying the struggle of withdrawal right from its opening lines: "There are no absolutes to human misery / Things can get worse." From there, thoughts of Frank race through his head as he copes with the paralyzing chills ("If this is hell, turn up the heat") and uncertainty ("Have you ever really faced fear / Like a butterfly in drying concrete?"), finding solace only in the dream whose flame was still barely flickering ("I just wanted to be good / Like the Beatles in Hollywood.")

Art had emerged from the darkness by summer 1993, ready to put a new band together and play rock and roll again. Among the new crop of Vancouver musicians pitching in was Sons of Freedom bassist Don Binns, guitarist-keyboardist Dave Genn of the band Dead Surf Kiss, and drummer Adam Drake of the band Stigmata. For Art, the simple goal of getting back onstage with other people played a major role in his recovery process, aided by the support of old and new friends alike, including the Lowest of the Low, who invited him to be a part of a two-night stand at Toronto's Lee's Palace in October.

Interview with the *Toronto Star*, October 14, 1993:
We haven't managed to learn any new stuff, mostly because what I want to do with the songs in the studio is kind of complicated. I wrote a couple albums' worth of material and threw them away. This has all happened since May, because before that I wasn't doing anything. I was sitting around because I really didn't know what to do. I mean, I didn't want to make any more demos or get another Canadian record deal. I got signed by these companies, and then I'd hear things like, sorry, you can't tour. Sorry, the time isn't right. You think things will happen when you sign to a major label, but the opposite happens. Hopefully, that's over now. It's a huge relief for me. I just look at artists I admire, they never made it until they were dead…or 50.

It's possible that these words sent a message to the Toronto music industry establishment, as in short order at least one of the major labels stepped forward to say it was prepared to take a chance on him again. The catalyst was Mike Roth, Sony Music Canada's head of A&R who, in 1993, got the go-ahead for one of his personal projects, an all-Canadian tribute album to Neil Young, with proceeds to be donated to Young's Bridge School, which developed innovative ways to educate severely impaired children. It was an era when tribute albums were common, and in many cases they revealed important connections between the new generation of "alternative rock" artists and influential artists from the '60s and '70s. Young had in fact been among the first to receive this treatment with the 1989 album *The Bridge* that featured contributions from Sonic Youth, Dinosaur Jr., Pixies, and others. Roth's list didn't have the same cachet, but it was more ambitious in its plan as a two-disc set, one all-acoustic and one all-electric. As that took shape in late 1992, Chris Wardman was hired to produce the debut album of a new Toronto band Jeff Rogers was managing called One Free Fall. The sessions that resulted in *Mud Creek* included a long workout on Young's "Cortez the Killer," and although its running time disqualified it for inclusion on Roth's project—now given the title *Borrowed Tunes*—the track did open the door for One Free Fall to be involved. During discussions with Roth, Wardman suggested that Art should also be involved in some capacity, and the concept quickly emerged of having Art and One Free Fall record something together.

"Chris really believed in Art, and I was aware of his body of work, so there was no hesitation in having him be a part of *Borrowed Tunes*," Roth said. It was decided that the most suitable song for Art to record was "Prisoners of Rock 'n Roll," from Young's 1987 album with Crazy Horse, *Life*. Made in the depths of Young's standoff with his then label boss, David Geffen, the song's unpolished fury, condensed into the shouted chorus "That's why we don't wanna be good," seemed an entirely apt reflection of Art's own experience, and fuelled by One Free Fall's punk-inspired energy, he delivered a stinging rendition.

Roth was suitably impressed and became curious to hear more. "Chris and I started talking a little bit about what Art had been through and he told me about some of the new material Art had been writing. Chris basically said, 'It would be great if someone just gave Art a chance.' By coincidence, we had a new president at Sony, Rick Camilleri, who was making a push to sign more Canadian artists. Once I'd heard some of the songs Art wanted to record, like 'Beatles in Hollywood,' it was easy to make a deal. We'd also just finished building a recording studio inside the Sony building in Toronto and were eager to have someone use it. So I approached Art and said, 'Here's what I can offer you, let's make an album and see what happens.' I think he was probably surprised that we were willing to work with him almost as a labour of love, but from my perspective, we had Leonard Cohen on the roster, so why shouldn't we have Art Bergmann as well?"

By the time *Borrowed Tunes* reached stores in the summer of 1994, recording was fully under way for the album that would become *What Fresh Hell Is This?*, with its title taken from a phrase most often attributed to the American writer Dorothy Parker, who is said to have deployed it frequently as an expression of her generally pessimistic view of life. Art adapted it for his purposes on the song "Some Fresh Hell," a rigid attempt at Bowie-esque post-punk that took direct aim at those in control of the illicit drug trade, making fortunes through keeping addicts enslaved to the product—"You turn your friends into your clientele / Like a vampire newlywed / Now you're needing some fresh little hell / Because you're all nearly dead."

Another song demoed was "Buried Alive," a heart-wrenching ballad with additional lyrics from Sherri that brought the agony of withdrawal back into sharp focus. There was also "Stop the Time," a half-whispered portrait of urban paranoia from the view of someone on a daily bus commute, and "In Betweens," a demonstration of Art's undiminished skills at writing taut, catchy power pop. Although "In Betweens" possessed all the elements of a potential radio single, that job fell to "Contract," a raging rocker on which Art unabashedly spat out his contempt for standard business practices. "Yeah, I dig my own grave for you / Be a total slave for you / Go around the world for you / Create a monster and bring it too." Mike Roth, for one, loved the irony of releasing it as a single, if only as an example that Sony Canada was home to more than just Celine Dion. "I think everyone at the company expected Art to make statements like that, so there were never any expectations of having a hit single," Roth said. "The feeling was that having Art on the roster sent a message to the wider industry that Sony wasn't just a label for artists who sold tons of records. At that point, we were seriously getting into the artist development game. So, looking back, I like to believe that the deal we had was beneficial to both parties."

As with the previous two records Chris Wardman had produced, the proper sessions for *What Fresh Hell Is This?* were completed efficiently over the course of a few weeks, despite taking place in a studio no one had been in before. "By then, I'd come to understand how complex Art's songwriting really was," Wardman said. "When we'd first started working together, my mindset would be 'Great, it'll be three-chord songs played really loud,' and then he'd come in and play me these really nuanced songs with minor chords in funny places. To record a song like 'Contract' was easy, but with everything else, I was always listening for the potential in each song, and approaching the production from that standpoint. The players were a big part of that too, especially Dave Genn, who was brilliant on keyboards."

As Roth recalled, "It was probably a strange feeling for everybody to be in that corporate environment, but they would often work all night and in the morning we would come in and listen to what they'd done. Art would occasionally give me some friendly ribbing, like 'Oh no, here comes the A&R guy, what's he gonna say?' But my response was always 'This is great, keep doing what you're doing.' I remember it being a really joyful time, and they made an incredible record."

In the end, after Wardman had added some psychedelic textures to it, the demo version of "Beatles in Hollywood" was deemed worthy of being used, and it was slotted in as the album's opening track. There was also the welcome addition of "Guns and Heroin," which had languished since the Poisoned sessions. As the producer, Wardman tried to focus solely on making these tracks as musically compelling as possible and letting the lyrics speak for themselves. "I didn't want to get into the weeds when it came to Art's lyrics," he said. "From time to time, Art would offer more background about them, but I think generally it was pretty clear what the songs were about. They were all so personal that I never wanted to interfere with that part of his creative process."

Interview with *Billboard*, March 11, 1995:

My wife Sherri talked me into re-recording ["Guns and Heroin"] because of the whole drug thing today in Vancouver with contracts, hit men, drugs and music. The song is still apropos. The guy who inspired it was later charged along with two others for killing this heiress. I'd come down every once in a while, and I'd feel weird, but a lot of creativity came out of that period. But it becomes such a death trip. It draws on all of your resources. You reduce everything to one problem every day, which is a huge problem. Still, there's something to be said about [drugs]. Look at these guys like Eric Clapton and Pete Townshend who are now clean and don't write very good music anymore.

Reviving "Guns and Heroin" also made a bold statement on how drugs were tearing apart not only the Vancouver music community, but, more visibly, the Seattle music scene just to the south. On April 8, 1994, the entire world was shocked to learn that Nirvana's Kurt Cobain—whose heroin addiction was common knowledge—had taken his own life with a shotgun, and in his suicide note had referenced Neil Young's famous line "It's better to burn out than to fade away." Being almost a generation removed from Cobain seemed to give Art a broader perspective on the situation when he was inevitably asked about how it may have impacted his work. Although he had no personal connection to Cobain, Art went on record that he considered them to be cut from the same cloth.

Interview with *Maclean's*, February 20, 1995:

People talk about my legend, how I've outlived it and all that crap. But all I've done is live to the best of my ability, which is moment to moment. My material comes from desperate living, which I get kudos for. And the fans who come out seem to know every word, which feels good, but it doesn't pay the rent. I'm just a writhing mass of contradictions. I'm here with the biggest record company in the world, yet I've been out there for so long that it's kind of hard to tie me up and point me in one direction. At least I've promised not to pull a Hindenburg until this one's run its course.

When *What Fresh Hell Is This?* was released in February 1995 on the Sony subsidary label Epic Records, the company did initially live up to its commitment to deploy its promotional resources, lining up interviews with major Canadian media outlets and paying for a bare-bones performance video for "Contract." Art and the band embarked on a Canadian club tour in the spring, but by its conclusion, shakeups at Sony were once again leaving Art on the outside looking in. "I think it was a classic case of the people at the label who loved you and championed you not having their jobs a year later," Wardman said. "Suddenly, there's this new group of people with no connection to the project being assigned to work it, and there just wasn't any enthusiasm there."

Things for Art were eerily starting to resemble the new film Bruce McDonald was shooting in 1995. *Hard Core Logo* was based on Michael Turner's novel about a fictional Vancouver punk band attempting a comeback while coping with each member's vastly different personal problems. The story opened with Hard Core Logo's singer, Joe Dick—played with pure conviction by Headstones vocalist Hugh Dillon—organizing a benefit concert for his mentor, Bucky Haight, who had become a recluse somewhere in Western Canada after supposedly being shot. The concert included explosive live performances by several Vancouver punk luminaries, including Art, but as the film unfolded, it vividly captured for the first time the harsh reality of life as an independent Canadian touring musician.

Yet, by the time *Hard Core Logo* hit theatres the following year, Art had been afforded one last moment of triumph by Sony—at least, that's how it appeared on the surface. In 1995 the Juno Awards created a new category, best alternative album, in response to rock music's recent evolution. The following year, *What Fresh Hell Is This?* was nominated alongside the debut album *Fluke* by Rusty, the band One Free Fall had morphed into, as well as excellent offerings by the Inbreds, the Super Friendz, and Hardship Post that sufficiently represented the national indie rock community. Both Art's age and the fact that he was signed to a major label seemed to make him the odd man out, so when he was announced as the winner during the non-televised portion of the gala held at Hamilton's Copps Coliseum, the surprise he and Sherri felt was entirely genuine.

"We were staying with the guys from Rusty, and we thought for sure they were going to win," Sherri said. "We loved those guys, so it was great that we got to all sit at the same table and have a good time together. When they said Art had won, we were really shocked. I looked at him, he looked

Hard Core Logo live shoot at the Commodore Ballroom, 1995, with Ziggy Sigmund on guitar. (PAUL CLARKE)

at me, and we were both going, 'What the fuck?' Art hadn't prepared a speech, so he went up to get the award and said something about dedicating it to his dead dad. I actually think some people booed. It was the weirdest thing."

What went unspoken was that Art had been informed that very day that Sony would not be asking for another album from him. "We'd received the news earlier that day, so winning the Juno really meant nothing," Sherri said. "I mean, was it going to get us another album? No. It was just a kick in the balls. I felt terrible for Art, but on the other hand I couldn't be angry with the people at Sony who had been working directly with him, because they were all completely supportive. Other people who didn't know Art, and didn't know how to market his music, made this decision. It really put us in this incomprehensible position of being back at square one at a moment when the industry had just acknowledged how great he was."

> In all honesty, I didn't think people would take to [*What Fresh Hell Is This?*], and of course people didn't. The style's all over the map. It was just a case of "Oh, here's another record deal. I'm stuck in the middle of Sony Corporation, recording more songs—I think I'll shoot up in the washroom!" It's nice to be with a record company, it's like a security blanket. "I need a cab ride, I gotta pick up my lyrics somewhere." They get you a cab, and fifty bucks later you're across town at some weirdo's house buying dope.

CHAPTER 11

CONFESSING
UNDER TORTURE

SHERRI MADE THE DECISION to clean up at the start of 1997, and both she and Art were determined to get through it together somehow. "Everyone I knew in Vancouver was a heroin addict, and a lot of us chose to get clean at the same time," she said. "It was harder for us because NA [Narcotics Anonymous] reminded me, and I think Art too, of the religious indoctrination that was forced upon us when we were growing up. 'Admit you're powerless'—no fucking way. I went to ninety-three meetings in ninety days before I gave up. I imagine Art and I probably talked each other out of it. We used to say, 'We'll be sick for seven days and then we'll never be sick again,' but man, is that ever hard. Some people think withdrawal is like the flu, but I could handle the flu standing on my head. Withdrawal is way worse.

"So in January 1997 I went to stay at my best friend's house in Calgary. Why I picked January to kick, I have no idea, but she and her husband had each quit, so it was a safe place for me to be. Art was living with his mother because we'd been evicted from our apartment in Vancouver."

Sherri believed the eviction stemmed from the couple being unable to receive welfare because of the publicity Art had garnered from the Juno win. From there, they had both fallen back into addiction by the end of 1996, and this time there were fewer lifelines to grab on to. The Lowest of the Low's manager, Frank Weipert, had taken responsibility for Art's business affairs, but following the Sony meltdown, he fully shifted his attention to his new clients, the Matthew Good Band, who had drafted in Art's keyboardist, Dave Genn, on guitar. Art was able to earn a little money by hosting a weekly Monday-night jam session at a Vancouver club called the Gate, a gig that was certainly beneath him, but as he'd demonstrated throughout his life, he felt no shame in doing whatever was necessary to earn a living. Stories even began circulating that he had sold the Juno statuette for heroin, something Sherri disputed, albeit with a caveat. "We never sold the Juno, but it was used as collateral," she said.

At some point during this period, Art was contacted by Frank Davies, the British-born Canadian music industry veteran who, in 1970, became the first independent label owner in the country to forge a distribution deal with a major, in his case Capitol/EMI. Davies also had success as a record producer, with his credits including Crowbar's "Oh What a Feeling," the song generally regarded as the first "CanCon" hit single, after the federal government implemented its quotas on cultural industries. Throughout the '70s, Davies continued to boost Capitol's roster of homegrown artists—including his most significant signing, Tom Cochrane & Red Rider—while building relationships with Capitol's US reps to give these artists a foothold in the American market. In 1982, Davies was named president of powerhouse music publisher ATV's Canadian division, a job he held until the entire company was purchased by Michael Jackson in 1986. That prompted him to start his own company, The Music Publisher (TMP), which in short order amassed thousands of songs by Canadian writers to which he administered the rights. In Davies's view, Art's estimated 135-song body of work—part of which Grant McDonagh had assembled in 1995 on the first Young Canadians CD compilation, *No Escape*—seemed a natural addition to his catalogue.

"[Art] was looking for some help personally and all of that, financially and everything, and we thought we may be able to help," Davies told the Vancouver *Province*'s Mike Roberts at the time. "Unfortunately, he didn't own the rights he thought he did, which was very disappointing, actually, to us and I think to him, too. I really wouldn't want to get into details on that because that really would be Art's sort of private business and I wouldn't like to do that. It was just a pity it never came to pass."

> **Suffice to say, [TMP] offered me $1,000. I didn't even dignify them with a response.**

In Sherri's recollection, "Art considered selling his publishing mainly so we could keep this apartment we wanted. It was a bad idea, but at that point we were getting a little desperate. We lived for a while in this booze can that had a skateboard ramp and a stage. The owners were kind enough to let us live behind the stage for a couple of months while we got our shit together. Then, when we managed to get the apartment, Art was contacted about selling his publishing, and the initial offer was for ten grand. But later it turned out they could only offer $1,000 for half the publishing on *What Fresh Hell Is This?*"

She added: "I always suspected that someone had taken out a life insurance policy on Art too. Some people were just waiting for him to die, literally, so they could fuck him over. One time when we cleaned up, a guy from NA would come whenever Art would play solo and stand on the stage, because people would buy him drinks, rusty nails or whatever, and line them up in front of him. These people wanted to see Art flip out and smash his guitar. That was the Art Bergmann they wanted to see, the crazy guy. He actually hated doing those acoustic shows because he had real anxiety about going onstage. So he'd have a drink for courage, which would help, until five drinks later, when it wouldn't. But there would be some nights when he was feeling good, playing the Town Pump or somewhere, and he would be just riveting."

Art laboured on into the winter as Sherri got straight in Calgary, until one day he received a call from Chris Houston, now living in Toronto, who proposed they do some shows together. Art met Sherri in Calgary, and they both departed for Toronto, little knowing what lay ahead. "I'd been hearing things about what Art was going through, so it seemed to me like it might be a good idea for him to get out of town," Houston said. "I talked to my friend Donnie Blais about setting up a little Ontario tour for Art and I to do, and Donnie got plane tickets for Art and Sherri."

Blais was a well-known figure in the Ontario punk community, specifically in Hamilton, where he had worked closely with Houston's band the Forgotten Rebels, as well as Teenage Head and others, promoting shows and taking on management duties whenever necessary. He'd opened a club on Queen Street West in Toronto called the Generator, which for a brief time in the late '90s became a haven for the city's punk and alternative rock scenes. "The night Art arrived, I remember Donnie picking us up and Art worrying that we were going to miss last call," Houston said. "But of course, with Donnie owning the bar, he'd commanded that all the drinks be set up when we got there. Then I remember Art walking around the empty Generator saying, 'When are they going to get wise to my ways?'"

Blais, for his part, didn't think twice about assisting someone he considered a Canadian music icon. "There was something really endearing about Art," Blais said. "He was kind of broken at the time, and seeing him that way really got to me. Here was one of the most brilliant guys I'd ever met, who should have been doing so much more, and getting the attention for it he deserved."

Assuming their stay in Toronto would only last as long as the tour, Sherri resisted adapting to their new environment at the outset. "We arrived on February 14, 1997, and I hated Toronto at first. There was garbage and dog shit everywhere, and I just kept thinking, 'My God, what have we done?' We stayed for a while with Ken MacNeil from Rusty before we moved in with Donnie Blais, who was so kind and generous to us. We never made enough money to move back west, so eventually I got to love being there."

After doing a couple of warm-up gigs at the Generator, Art and Houston started venturing out into the surrounding territory, not really knowing what to expect. In previewing the March 1 date at La Luna in Hamilton, the *Spectator*'s Bruce Mowat wrote: "Over the past few months, Bergmann has been performing as a solo acoustic artist, something he started doing when it became apparent to him his back-up band wasn't going to stick around someone without the backing of a major label. These, however, aren't your standard garden-variety unplugged shows.

"During these shows, Bergmann makes a point of not only giving the audience an overview of his career, but also detailed dissections of the songs in question, sometimes explaining midway through the performance what in-jokes and musical references are alluded to in the song's melody and lyrics. There's also a sprinkling of covers from the artists that shaped Bergmann's music, including selections from the songbooks of Neil Young, Gram Parsons, and The Replacements."

At the start of April, Art was invited by Toronto roots rockers Skydiggers to open two nights for them at the Birdland Cabaret in Halifax, a trip that marked the farthest east he'd yet travelled in Canada.

> **Interview with the Halifax *Daily News*, April 4, 1997:**
> I'm hoping that shows like these will help establish me as a songwriter in people's minds, instead of just an old punk. It's been working. People can hear most of the words that I'm singing, and it gives me a chance to break

off and tell the audience where the songs are coming from, what their influences are. Actually, [performing solo] was really scary the first couple of times I did it. Having a band is like having a facade, a mask almost. And to strip all of that away is like being naked. And since all of my songs are pretty honest—brutally honest, sometimes—it makes you feel even more vulnerable.

The following week, Art and Houston were back playing around southern Ontario, including a Wednesday night stop at a bar in Kitchener called Mrs. Robinson's, where an indifferent response provoked some of Art's old fury. When the audience's attention waned after the first few songs, Art fell into a pattern of downing a gin and tonic, hurling the glass against the back wall, where it smashed into shards, and calmly playing the next song. The night turned into a bizarre form of cabaret that left some in attendance questioning Art's state of mind.

Interview with the Halifax *Daily News*, April 4, 1997:
I don't trust people who don't drink. But all those stories are things out of my past that I use in my songs, but that all the journalists try to pick up on. I don't think I've ever really had a serious problem. I'm not saying that I can't be nasty, but I don't put the boots to anybody until the knife's been twisted into my back. All my moves are strictly defensive.

By the summer of 1997, it was becoming obvious that Art and Sherri wouldn't be able to move back to Vancouver anytime soon. Blais was still happy to provide them space to live in his basement, and the couple got along well with his family. They were also fortunate to be accepted into a methadone treatment program, which Sherri said completely changed their outlook. "I was a little hesitant at first because one thing my father told me before he died was that my mother was a methadone addict when I was born. That seemed to explain things I'd heard—that as a baby I would sleep from 4 in the afternoon to 7 in the morning without waking up, which is pretty frightening to think about now. But doing that treatment turned out to be the best thing for us."

Meanwhile, Art spent free time during the day doing basic clean-up work at the Generator. "It was just something to keep him occupied," Blais said. "He never complained about anything and I never pushed him. He just needed something to focus on when he wasn't thinking about playing music. It may have been that year when we were one of the venues hosting Canadian Music Week or North by Northeast showcases, and I'll never forget a few young musicians coming up to me and saying, 'Man, that guy sweeping the floor over there really looks like Art Bergmann.' I might have told them that it was, but I generally didn't want to interfere with Art's recovery at that point."

Ominously, however, Art's songwriting didn't provide the form of therapy that it once did. It seemed the previous two years had been so traumatic that even attempting to put it down on paper was too painful. Only one new song, "Hung Out to Dry," emerged fully formed during this period, a bleak reflection of his recent experiences in the music industry, played as a bitter-sweet waltz.

> In the old days I got so sick of writing songs that it made me write more songs. I was throwing away so much stuff. What's the fucking point? Around then, I decided to wait until there was a gun to my head and some money on the line before I said anything into a microphone. It became the old "confess under torture." I pride myself on functioning. All this stuff about me being in rehab all the time is a load of bullshit. Someone came up with that just to get writers to write about my dope habit. They latched on to that like a bone when it came out—"April '93, Art went into detox." I've kicked so many habits. According to them, I've gone maybe five or six times since then. What's new? It's part of the process.

As might be expected, Art's presence in Toronto soon attracted the interest of the city's first generation of punk fans, some of whom had moved on to more business-oriented ventures. Among them was Jan Haust, who ran the label Other People's Music, best known for its "Hole of Fame" series that reissued the work of Toronto's best-known early punk bands, such as the Viletones, the Demics, the Ugly, the Mods, the 'B' Girls, and the Forgotten Rebels. It complemented his primary interest in archiving Toronto's rock and roll history, with the technical aspects of that pursuit handled by Haust's partner Peter J. Moore, who had his own mastering studio, the E Room, but was better known as the sonic mastermind behind Cowboy Junkies' breakthrough album *The Trinity Session*, recorded with a single Calrec ambisonic microphone at the Church of the Holy Trinity in downtown Toronto.

Haust couldn't pass up the opportunity of working with Art, and extended an offer to record what amounted to his acoustic set for a proposed Other People's Music release. As in his early dealings with Quintessence Records, Art took it on faith that Haust's primary motivation was to get the music out to those who would most appreciate it, so not much time was spent discussing financial details. It was merely agreed that Art would turn up at Moore's house with his acoustic guitar on a scheduled date and record as if he were playing a club show.

The songs for what became *Design Flaw* were captured in Moore's kitchen, the room that served as his makeshift home studio. Art ran through his best material, starting with "Our Little Secret" and continuing with "Faithlessly Yours" and "If She Could Sing." However, the overall tone ultimately tilted toward the darker corners of his solo body of work, with the new interpretations of "Hospital Song," "Buried Alive," and "More Blue Shock" making a strong case that it was entirely possible for Art to re-emerge as a Leonard Cohen–esque figure whose songs were as powerful in the starkest of settings as they were when played by a full rock band. With "Hung Out to Dry" fitting the theme of the session, Art also chose to record Gram Parsons's "Sin City," the mystical country song that had remained an obsession of his since he'd first heard Parsons and the Flying Burrito Brothers play it in 1969. From its opening lines "This old town's filled with sin / It'll swallow you in / If you've got some money to burn," it now in many ways reflected Art's journey and the temptations that had come along the way. The fact that he had overcome them while Parsons had died from a heroin overdose in 1973, at age twenty-seven, only added gravity to Art's performance, and enhanced his new-found view of himself as a storyteller.

Haust and Moore sat on the tape for several months while debating how best to present it to the world. Haust eventually felt the album would acquire more cachet if he asked British guitarist Chris Spedding to overdub some parts. Haust had established a relationship with Spedding during the 1980s, when Other People's Music secured a Canadian release for his solo albums *Enemy Within* and *Cafe Days*, put out in Europe on the respected French punk label New Rose Records. Spedding had come up through the UK rock scene of the late '60s as somewhat of a guitar prodigy, and went on to a career as an in-demand session player while occasionally scoring a domestic solo hit single. His punk credentials were firmly established in 1976, when he produced the Sex Pistols' initial three-song demo—possibly the same tape Art heard that year—and again a couple of years later when he formed a long-term collaboration with New York punk turned rockabilly revivalist Robert Gordon.

Spedding agreed to come to Toronto in November 1997, first laying down electric guitar parts on all of Art's tracks at Moore's house, then accompanying Art for a show at the Generator a few days later. Being a consummate professional, Spedding got along well with Art, never overstepping his bounds, but in the aftermath left little indication that a creative partnership might develop beyond that.

The fact was, Art still had a long way to go, and he was dealt another emotional blow when his ever-supportive mother, Edith, died on February 27, 1998, at the age of eighty-two. It would take until October of that year for Haust to release *Design Flaw*, and by then Donnie Blais had closed the Generator and opened a new restaurant and bar on College Street called Rancho Relaxo. Art and Sherri found new accommodations in the nearby Little Portugal neighbourhood, though Art continued to work for Blais at the new spot, doing menial tasks and sometimes kitchen duty. Like the Generator, Rancho maintained a busy live music schedule, and the pattern repeated of young touring musicians often looking quizzically at the guy picking up their empty beer bottles and asking one another, "Is that Art Bergmann?"

However, Rancho still afforded Art the opportunity to get onstage regularly, and it was there that the celebration was held when the time finally came to unveil *Design Flaw*. Spedding happened to be in town again, producing an album for Dee Dee Ramone that Haust had agreed to release, and gladly reprised his role with Art at Rancho. *Design Flaw* was received as well as any independent Canadian album could expect at that time—meaning good reviews but limited sales and airplay—but it did appear to give Art a shot of energy he had been hoping for. He booked some solo shows in the west, and suggested in an interview with the *Toronto Star*'s Ben Rayner that he wanted to round up some Vancouver musicians, bring them back to Toronto, and start playing loud rock and roll again as soon as possible.

Interview with the *Edmonton Sun*, November 13, 1998:
I've had writer's block for a couple of years, [but] there's lots still left in me. I don't know what happiness is, necessarily, but I think the reason we're alive is to come to terms with that. I'm getting to the point of almost a reliable income again. I'm making a living. I don't want anything else anymore.

Sherri was also starting to feel at home. "After we got our apartment in Little Portugal, it was great. We got a dog, and we started meeting all of these wonderful people in the neighbourhood—actors, writers, schoolteachers—and they all became our friends. It was a struggle financially, but we had a lot of people rooting for us."

Unfortunately, the financial struggle persisted because Other People's Music was incapable of promoting *Design Flaw* properly. Rather than serving as the first step in a full-fledged comeback, the album was ultimately perceived as another of Jan Haust's vanity projects. In autumn

Sherri (right) with daughter Naomi, 1994. (MARK DUFFY)

2000, in part to remedy this situation however he could, Chris Houston took it upon himself to produce the CD *Vultura Freeway*, which compiled and remastered all of Art's initial solo demos recorded with Cec English in early 1984. It was a worthy companion piece to *Design Flaw*, and filled an important gap in Art's overall story, but again, without the backing of a major record label, it was released into a void.

Still, having a contented life in Toronto was a sufficient trade-off, until word came from Red Deer, Alberta, that Sherri's daughter, Naomi, was pregnant with her first child, a daughter to be named Zoe. Given the rigid upbringing Sherri had endured with her adopted family, which led directly to her contentious relationship with Naomi's father, it became imperative for Sherri to be as close as she could in order to offer all the necessary support.

"That was a really hard decision we had to make about leaving Toronto, but I wanted to make sure my granddaughter grew up without being surrounded by this right-wing view of life like I was," Sherri said. She found an affordable house located on a large farm in Rocky View County, near Airdrie, just north of Calgary, and it became their unlikely new home at the end of 2005. When word got out about Art's move, some *Hard Core Logo* fans immediately started drawing parallels to the character Bucky Haight's circumstances, but for Art, the new, isolated location didn't precipitate what eventually became his own five-year exile from the music business. The reason for that was much more serious.

Even while in Toronto, Art started to sense his body doing strange things he hadn't felt before. His hands and feet would increasingly go numb, to the point where his family doctor sent him to a neurologist who determined that several discs in his spine were deteriorating. As Sherri explained, "After our first meeting with the neurologist, he said that Art needed surgery. We asked if we could think about it, and he said no, Art will be paralyzed by the time you come back."

> They went through my neck and put some titanium around my spinal cord, or else I would have been a paraplegic within a year. Too much pogoing at Subhumans shows. Seriously, though, I don't know what caused it, but it's gone all through my spine. I've got a lot of pain in my legs that comes and goes, but before the surgery I couldn't even walk.

Art's condition improved for a while following the surgery, but it was soon determined he had degenerative disc disease and osteoarthritis. More surgeries would be required, particularly if he had any hope of playing guitar. As Art adapted to this new reality news came that Ray Fulber was aiming to release the Bob Rock mixes of the 1986 Poisoned demos on CD, under the title *Lost Art Bergmann* through his own Bearwood Music label. For Fulber, who had the master tapes stored in his basement, it was a matter of putting them out before the elements rendered them completely unsalvageable. "I've lost different parts of my life for different reasons," Fulber said at the time of *Lost Art Bergmann*'s appearance in the spring of 2009. "Any one regret is not a good one, you know? And I just thought, I'm going to try to do this at the highest level. I found the same Studer machine that Bob Rock worked on, and I got a good mastering engineer and I found old photos." Yet, to ensure the best audio quality, Fulber had to attempt the risky process of baking the tapes in a food dehydrator, in order to burn off any residue that would impede playback. "If I didn't [do that], it would have been a shadowy, 'Oh yeah, that's kind of cool' curiosity, right? But I really wanted to try to get what I felt when I first heard [these mixes]."

Art consented to Fulber's plan to release the album, and despite the pain he was in, further agreed to come to Vancouver for a CD launch party on March 26, 2009, at Richard's on Richards that would essentially amount to a Poisoned reunion with Susann Richter and Taylor Nelson Little. Art and Sherri stayed at Fulber's house on the Sunshine Coast while the band, with Vancouver punk stalwart Tony "Baloney" Walker supplanting Art on guitar, got in a few rehearsals. The show was a sellout, with Art taking the stage to a loud ovation, wearing glasses and a sharply tailored blue suit and red shirt. Instead of a guitar, a stool and a podium were placed by his microphone, as if he were there to give a lecture, but both were rudely dispatched after the first song. Fuelled by a steady supply of beer and tequila, Art led the band through "Bound for Vegas," "The Junkie Don't Care," and other songs from that period, while taking potshots at some of his favourite targets, Canadian politicians and the music industry. From the audience's perspective, the night was a triumphant reminder of Art's stature in the Vancouver music scene, but it ultimately left him unsatisfied.

> Ray and Susann talked me into thinking I couldn't play [guitar] at all. That was a bitter day. In Toronto, it was no problem, so I'm not sure if it was old, bad relationships causing stress or what. I was up there with no guitar, and it really pissed me off. They wouldn't let anyone else jam with me either, they just wanted to focus on this one little slice of my career. I told them that I can't do that; there's more people I've played with longer that I wanted to get up onstage. Bob Rock wanted to jam, and somebody shut that down, I'm not sure who. As soon as we finished the set, it was the old 'Turn on the lights, turn up the fucking disco,' and it was over.

Despite the sour taste the show left in Art's mouth, the old guard in Vancouver got the presumed last hurrah they were expecting. Little did they know, however, that a month later Art would be back onstage in one of Toronto's most prestigious theatres, at the behest of one of the country's most admired young singer-songwriters. Art didn't realize it then, but it would be the moment when he could finally put the punk baggage behind him.

ULTIMATE FREEDOM

As the arrival of their fourth album, *Lost Channels*, approached in the spring of 2009, Toronto's Great Lake Swimmers set to work planning its release in a manner that would do justice to the record's lush, expansive sound. Like previous albums, the connection between the music and where it was performed was crucial to its overall concept; *Lost Channels* was recorded primarily at Singer Castle in New York's Thousand Islands region, where Lake Ontario begins feeding the Saint Lawrence River. It was also Great Lake Swimmers' first effort in a new deal with Nettwerk Records, and the critical response to *Lost Channels* would firmly cement GLS's status as one of Canada's most compelling folk-rock bands. They ultimately chose to debut the record on April 25 at an unusually formal Toronto venue, the Queen Elizabeth Theatre, located on the Exhibition Place grounds, with a capacity of twelve hundred. Because the venue boasted some of the best acoustics in the city, playing there marked an important milestone for the band, but leader Tony Dekker saw the show as a further opportunity to do something special.

Dekker first became aware of Art while attending Western University in London, Ontario, during the late '90s. He was involved with the campus radio station, CHRW, and became intrigued when others there started talking about Art coming to play a solo show on campus at the Grad Club. Dekker decided to drop in, without an inkling of what to expect. "He was very confrontational with the audience, and it felt like it could fall apart at any minute," Dekker recalled. "But it was amazing, and dangerous at the same time. I became an instant fan and went out and got all the albums. I think it was before *Design Flaw* had come out, and that became one of my favourites when I heard it."

As Art gradually faded from public view over the ensuing years, Dekker remained curious about his activities. Those thoughts were still in his mind when the *Lost Channels* launch show sold out months in advance, and GLS manager Phil Klygo told Dekker that Nettwerk had given them carte blanche to add whoever they wanted to the bill. Dekker mulled over which friends or up-and-coming bands might be appropriate, but couldn't help asking Klygo, "I wonder what Art Bergmann's doing?" Dekker said, "I was feeling like I was in a position to connect and possibly collaborate with people I really respected, so after Phil and I had that conversation, he went to work trying to find out where Art was. He eventually found him and Art agreed to come to Toronto, but somehow I think it was miscommunicated that the show was for my birthday and that's why I asked for him. To this day, I'm still not sure if Art thinks that was the reason."

Klygo added: "It kind of blew my mind when Tony brought up Art's name, because he certainly wasn't on anybody's radar. In fact, I think my response was 'Is he alive or dead?' But I did some digging, and it wasn't too hard to find a phone number for him. I think he was flattered to be asked, but he had never heard of Great Lake Swimmers, so his main question was 'Why me?'"

Art did his best to familiarize himself with Great Lake Swimmers' sound, realizing this was an opportunity to create a completely different experience than the Vancouver show the previous month. He called Chris Wardman, who gladly agreed to resume his role on guitar while putting together a band that could bring out the more rootsy aspects of Art's sound. Art played acoustic guitar this time, and backed by Wardman, Jason Sniderman on keyboards, Sammy Kohn of alt-rockers the Watchmen on drums, Bob Egan—then with Blue Rodeo— on pedal steel, and Jonny Kerr on bass, he was fully prepared to perform in a style and setting he had never attempted before.

Performing at Toronto's Queen Elizabeth Theatre, 2009.
(COURTESY CHRIS WARDMAN)

It all came off beautifully from Dekker's perspective, and although he didn't get to spend as much time with Art as he would have liked to before the show, that night was the start of a lasting friendship, from the moment when Art invited Dekker onstage to sing "Sin City" with him. "When I initially thought of having Art play, I assumed he would do it solo and it would kind of be like coming full circle from that first time I'd seen him," Dekker said. "But he had this incredible band, which I'm sure surprised some people—those who knew him, and likely those who had never heard his music before. It was supposed to be our band's night, but in the end I was just as happy to see Art onstage in front of that many people."

It was certainly an achievement Art could savour, as all he really had to look forward to back in Alberta was more painful physical therapy. Yet the spectre of his punk years still lingered. When Vancouver documentarian Susanne Tabata set out to make the film *Bloodied but*

Unbowed, the first comprehensive account of the Vancouver punk scene, she envisioned it revolving around the three distinct themes of Art's lyricism, Joe Keithley's perseverance, and Gerry Hannah's political activism. Art had no qualms about participating in the film, but much of the new footage Tabata shot, particularly a clip of Art introducing the Pointed Sticks at a Vancouver reunion show in August 2008, revealed the full effects of his arthritis for the first time to many who had lost touch with him. *Bloodied but Unbowed* premiered in May 2010 and continued to be showcased at film festivals over the next two years to generally glowing reviews, many of which specifically noted Art's appearance, as did the *Georgia Straight*, which wrote: "[There are] moments of painful poignancy (ex-Young Canadian Art Bergmann trying to make sense of where it all went wrong)." As someone who always thrived in the moment, Art was generally disturbed by how suddenly he was being relegated to the past. The film had now fully enshrined him as a "punk legend" for whatever that was worth, and given his circumstances at the time, it didn't seem like much.

Then, at the start of summer 2013, Sherri got word that her biological father, Jack Ivers, was in poor health. Although she desperately wanted to see him, the expense of an extended trip to Vancouver was beyond what she and Art could afford. However, with Art's strength continually returning, he proposed setting up a gig that would at the very least pay for them to get there and back.

Reunion with Tony Bardach, Zippy Pinhead and Randy Rampage, 2013. (ALEX WATERHOUSE-HAYWARD)

It also gave him the opportunity to follow up on his desire to play guitar in a rock and roll context again, and erase some of the bad memories of the Poisoned reunion. After a few calls, Art got commitments from bassist Kevin Lucks—whose former outfit No Exit earned the distinction in 1980 of being the first Vancouver punk band to release a full-length album—and drummer Adam Drake, who in turn enlisted his brother Steven, co-frontman of the well-known power pop band Odds, to play second guitar. The date of July 1 was booked at the WISE Hall, a multi-purpose performance space that served as a hub for a wide range of Vancouver cultural organizations, and Art and Sherri were able to arrive a week ahead to allow him to get in a half-dozen rehearsals.

On top of noting his physical state, many who hadn't seen him in the four years since the Poisoned show couldn't help acknowledging how much more introspective he'd become, something he admitted was a by-product of his new surroundings.

Interview with the *Toronto Star*, October 22, 2014:

I do a lot of reading and investigation into the human condition. If I want weird city life I can zip into Calgary, where I've found a band now. I kind of ignored the music business for all that time. Why I did that was because as soon as you approach success, whoever you're dealing with wants you to repeat yourself. That's not my modus operandi. I told Chris Wardman the other day, there's no point in not playing. You do what you do, just do it. Every four or five years I used to go through whole circles of friends, people who gave up art or music and got sucked in by their fucking mortgage and family and the career or job thing. It's so sad. People just melt into society at large. You've gotta live your life to the fullest. You get one life, why do you wanna get sucked into this brutal system? It's just unbelievable to me.

Although he still drank in moderation, being drug-free since his time in Toronto had also contributed to the change in Art's personality, as well as to his ability to focus on his music. As Steven Drake later commented, "Art tries to hide all the theoretical stuff he knows about chords and notes. He tries to make us think it is purely intuitive. This is not the case. He understands it all deeply and we were able to communicate musically."

Lucks helped out in his own way by suggesting Art take a natural pain medicine containing components of snake venom, much like traditional remedies that had been used to treat arthritis and inflammation in India and China for centuries. It did indeed give Art a much-needed boost to get through the rehearsals, while providing the band with a suitable name, Viper Juice. Another advantage was that Art's appearances in Vancouver were now covered by the media as rare events, and the WISE Hall show was deemed a success by both fans and critics, as he breathed new life into songs such as "Remember Her Name," "Message from Paul," and "Dirge No. 1." Art's old friend, the photographer Alex Waterhouse-Hayward, wrote on his blog: "There are at least two thoughts I came out with after the concert. One was that the audience and Bergmann's band have pumped him up with enthusiasm to come back and play at a larger venue. The other is that at 60, Bergmann has more brilliance to show us. I hope I am around to see and hear it."

Art did in fact return for another sold-out Vancouver show with Viper Juice at the Biltmore Cabaret on October 26, taking the stage in something approximating a Hugh Hefner–style smoking jacket, and pushing his stamina to its limit with as much pure abandon as he could muster. It all turned out to be a reflection of his reinvigorated passion to write, which continued to burn over the course of the coming winter.

What drew me back was the clock on my life and a need to get a few things I'd learned over my hiatus out of my head. But foremost, I wanted to see if I could make a bit of a living doing the only thing I know how, songwriting. I did not miss the gossiping, backstabbing business, I can tell you that much.

> We followed [the WISE Hall show] up with an October show and there were twice as many people, so I thought, 'Oh, why not?' All these years, I've always been writing and taking notes while I slaughter one history book after another, so I had tons of ideas and they just started to jell. I finally picked up a guitar again and just started playing it non-stop for eighteen months.

The first song to emerge was "Drones of Democracy," a long, minor-key guitar workout inspired by two Neil Young classics, "Cortez the Killer" and "Ohio." Over its grinding chords, Art intoned his thoughts on the culture of war that had led to the creation of previously unimaginable weapons capable of near-surgical destruction. It was unlike anything Art had written before in its free form and almost stream-of-consciousness feel, even though he later admitted to revising the lyrics mercilessly until he was satisfied. But in essence, the song was a glimpse into the effect that the sounds of traditional Indian music and the vast, arid sonic landscapes created by traditional North African players were having on him whenever he tuned into his favourite programs on Calgary's campus radio station, CJSW.

Another new song, "Company Store," was constructed around the ramshackle fury of Bob Dylan's initial forays into rock and roll, while lyrically paying homage to Tennessee Ernie Ford's immortal "Sixteen Tons." But while Ford had put himself into the boots of a beleaguered coal miner, Art expanded that notion to chastise society in general for selling out its values to corporate interests. We were all now "whores at the company store" in Art's estimation.

After completing two more songs, the long and lyrically dense "Ballad of a Crooked Man," which gave nods to revolutionaries from Robespierre to Lenin, and "Your Cold Appraising Eye," a lament for lives at the mercy of those who manipulate the financial markets—written almost in the style of a soul ballad that allowed Art to deliver one of his finest vocal performances—he was ready to return to the recording studio. In the course of familiarizing himself with the Calgary music community, Art had found a sympathetic ear in the form of Lorrie Matheson, a fixture of the scene since the early '90s, best known for his work with the alt-country band National Dust. He and Art shared a love of the Replacements and other raucous, roots-based rock and roll, and Matheson didn't hesitate to invite Art to lay down some tracks at his studio, Arch Audio, in the spring of 2014.

> Interview with *Exclaim!*, September 3, 2014:
> I called up Lorrie because he was the only guy I knew in Calgary, and he helped me out immensely. He got me into his studio even though he was under pressure to finish five albums. He said, we'll make it work. I put him through the wringer. I said, it'll just be three days, but it ended up being a lot more than that. That is about the time Phil Klygo stepped in and said he'd give me a bit of money to do it. And I mean a little bit, as we did this record for less than $2,000. But it has been a tortuous process, I must say.

Along with managing Great Lake Swimmers, Klygo ran the Toronto-based label (wee-werk), which had helped launch the careers of other forward-thinking roots-rock acts, such as Elliott Brood, FemBots, and the Burning Hell. But since his first encounter with Art, Klygo had dug into Art's back catalogue and became intrigued with the possibility of reissuing some of the harder-to-find items. "I wasn't really looking to sign new bands at that time, because I had enough on my plate, but as I heard more of Art's music and learned about his dealings with the industry, I began feeling like we shared a lot of similarities," Klygo said. "So we maintained regular contact, and one day Art said, 'I've got some new stuff, would you like to hear it?' I said, 'Of course,' and that led to putting out the first EP."

Songs for the Underclass, composed of the four songs recorded with Matheson, was released at the end of August 2014 and caught much of the Canadian music media by surprise. On its cover was a tinted head shot of Art, his face showing the tell-tale lines of age, though its most striking feature was Art's green fatigue cap adorned with the Chinese Communist Party's red star. The overall symbolism of the packaging designed by David Cran sent a powerful political message, but it was backed up by the songs, all of them stinging indictments—in one way or another—of the dark side of capitalism.

From a musical standpoint, Matheson had done an excellent job of bringing in the right musicians to suit the feel of each song, with the masterstroke being Emily Burrowes's supporting vocal on "Your Cold Appraising Eye," which accentuated the emotional resonance of Art's performance. In a marked reversal from *Design Flaw*, critics were quick to take notice. Writing for the *Huffington Post*, Jeff Rose-Martland stated: "Good protest songs—the ones that endure—never preach to the choir. They don't rally the converted. They never tell you what to do, just that something should be done. Good protest songs force you to think, to consider. Art Bergmann reveals his mastery of the genre with the 4 song EP *Songs for the Underclass*. He shows you the screwed-up world and you have to decide how to deal with it."

Buoyed by the positive response, Art undertook a brief round of shows in his primary strongholds: Vancouver, Victoria, Calgary, Toronto, Hamilton, and Ottawa. He now had a network of loyal musicians in BC, Alberta, and Ontario capable of playing whatever was required from his catalogue, which eliminated some of the stress of touring and complemented Klygo's skill at getting things done on shoestring budgets. Tony Dekker also chipped in again by doing solo opening sets for the Ontario shows. "That was when I got to know him a little better," Dekker said. "We had more time to talk, and he would share these incredible stories about playing shows with the Dead Kennedys and other bands from that period. But I was most impressed by how politically and socially energized he was. I think that's the through-line with all of his work, no matter what genre label someone might put on it. That's why I don't really like to think of Art's music in terms of genre—it's more like an aesthetic. I can see now that he was a part of this group of artists, including Jello Biafra and others, who did what they did with a sense altruism, and not just to cause chaos."

Performing at the Calgary Folk Music Festival, July 26, 2014. (Phil Klygo)

Robert Catherall, in reviewing the Commodore Ballroom show for *Discorder* magazine, seemed to pick up on that idea as well. When Art caved in to the crowd's demand to hear "Hawaii," Catherall noted, the band played the song at a deliberately slow tempo before attacking "Bound for Vegas" at full throttle. Catherall concluded: "For a man who seemed haunted, even tortured, by how much he has to say about the current, and future state of affairs, the enigmatic figure nevertheless maintained his reputation as the local prince of punk. For on this night, where troop rallying newcomers were juxtaposed with drawn out age-old hits, Bergmann's ideas were delivered unapologetically, and in a manner of extremes."

Art continued to write at a prodigious pace into 2015, with the assurance that the rug wasn't going to be pulled out from under him by a record company. In fact, by that point, the music industry as he had known it no longer existed. Hip-hop was now the dominant genre, and the rise of streaming services meant the loss of millions in retail sales. The days of major labels spending extravagantly on artist development and promotion were long gone, and those labels that were even willing to take a chance on music deemed "alternative" most often cut distribution deals with independent labels or with artists directly. Perhaps most tellingly, the notion of artists "selling out," which Art had mocked with "Bound for Vegas" and "Contract," had almost entirely vanished. No longer did anyone begrudge artists for licensing their music for film and television or, for that matter, advertising. With so little money on the table, artists were now almost obligated to go after it any way they could.

On stage at the Commodore Ballroom,
September 6, 2014. (Bob Hanham)

Yet, for once, Art was in the advantageous position of having a team of people on his side with no agenda beyond helping him pursue his reconstituted musical vision and navigate through this new world. With eight songs singled out from his growing cache of new material, Art once again turned to Lorrie Matheson to bring them to life in autumn 2015. The intent was to expand upon the sound and themes of *Songs for the Underclass*, which proved to be a challenge given that these were Art's most complex and emotionally charged songs to date.

Signs of this were apparent in Art's title for the album, *The Apostate*, by definition a person who renounces their religious or political beliefs on principle. While it remained easy for him to take aim at big targets like government corruption, warmongering, and corporate greed, the changes in society just beginning to penetrate mainstream consciousness at that moment—climate change acceptance, the MeToo movement, and Indigenous truth and reconciliation—deeply affected Art's mindset and seemed to reflect the evolution of his musical approach, which he now liked to describe as "country and eastern."

Any traces of simple, three-chord rock and roll were harder to pick out, with only "Live It Up" fitting that bill. With its crunchy groove propelling the hook "Live it up, you're gonna die!"—sung with perverse glee by a gang chorus—the song served as a meditation on aging, as well as an ironic counterpoint to artists like his beloved Rolling Stones, who were still filling arenas based on youthful fantasies. However, most of the material on *The Apostate* dispensed with such inside jokes, focusing instead on the roots of injustice and the musical templates laid out in "Drones of Democracy" and "Ballad of a Crooked Man."

One of the stories that dominated the news in Canada in 2015 was the downfall of CBC host Jian Ghomeshi, after he was charged with sexual assault, based on the testimony of three women. It was a prelude to the global MeToo movement, and inflamed many Canadians, especially when Ghomeshi received a full acquittal. Art was among those infuriated, and his response was "Cassandra," titled after the mythological figure who was cursed with seeing truthful visions of the future, but whose prophecies were never believed. Opening with the devastating line "I'll never know how it feels to be a woman / When all your love breaks on silence and falls," Art refused to take the position of a character and instead faced his own reckoning.

> Cassandra was a princess of Troy. Apollo took her under his wing and guided her gifts of perception and prophecy. When he had finished, he expected her to fuck him—been there. She refused, he raped her, then he spit in her mouth as a curse that, although being a prophetess, she wouldn't be believed. All women have been Cassandra at one point in their lives—that spit of Apollo. What to do with violent men? Sherri got it right for me after I made the mistake on first writing that I thought I might know how it would feel to be the woman. We think we are more civilized than other cultures.

By 2015, through the efforts of the Idle No More movement and other protests, a lot of Canadians were also reckoning with the country's past and current treatment of Indigenous peoples. Although the fight for Indigenous rights had never abated since Canada's founding in

1867, the coming of social media had given it a much broader platform, allowing many to reach a better understanding of broken treaties, uninhabitable conditions on reserves, and crimes committed against children at residential schools. Art attempted to capture the big picture on "Pioneers," a sprawling, ten-minute epic highlighted by the work of multi-instrumentalist Paul Rigby, a new, trusted Vancouver collaborator known for his work with Neko Case. Over a backdrop of haunting soundscapes, Art painted an entirely different mythology of the west, one where there were no heroes, just the countless innocent victims whose blood paid the cost of western expansion.

Bringing it all into sharper modern context, Art wrote the stark acoustic ballad "The Legend of Bobby Bird" to close out the album, as a tribute to the ten-year-old Saskatchewan boy who in 1969 ran away from his remote residential school and wasn't seen again until his remains were found years later. It took many more years until DNA testing could make a positive identification. Art was moved to write the song after reading a newspaper article about Bird's short life, and once he felt confident with the results, he approached Bird's family for their approval.

> I wanted to have him represent all of the vanished kids. I wanted him to become a legend where they all chose nature instead of going back to those prisons. They'd rather just disappear instead of going back. That's where the legend comes in; they joined the spirits of the earth instead of the non-spirit world of those brutal schools.
>
> I needed to get [his family's] blessing to make sure I got it right. They didn't want to use the word *Cree*. This is very important to them. *Cree* is not how they talk about themselves, *Cree* is a colonial construct. So I had to learn some words. It was difficult, but they taught me how to say them and I hope I got them right in the song. It's been very educational on my part. When I play it, I barely get through it without weeping. So I would like this country to listen, think, and learn more about what happened. I want them to hear this song and weep, and get down on their knees in remorse, even if they say "the sins of our fathers."

The following year, the Tragically Hip's Gord Downie and graphic novelist Jeff Lemire brought the story of another '60s residential school escapee, Chanie Wenjack, to the public consciousness with their project *Secret Path*. It coincided with the shocking news of Downie's inoperable brain tumour, and as part of his final act Downie took every opportunity to raise awareness of Wenjack's story through the Hip's emotional farewell tour and through the Gord Downie & Chanie Wenjack Fund for programs aimed at reconciliation between Indigenous and non-Indigenous peoples. Although it overshadowed what Art had done with "The Legend of Bobby Bird," there could be no question that it was all contributing to a larger conversation about Canada's previously suppressed history.

> This is one thing I can do in my life that will have a positive effect. I've never had any power. I dealt with awful, awful people in the music business, and now this little thing without all those people involved is happening and it's really gratifying.

The Apostate, with its cover depicting Art in a Buddhist meditative pose, was released on (weewerk) in April 2016. It was praised across the board in Canada, and that summer was named to the long list for the Polaris Music Prize, the award for the best Canadian album of the year as determined by critics.

After performing another handful of well-received shows in select cities, as he'd done in support of *Songs for the Underclass*, Art settled back into life on the farm, confident that he could now work at his own pace. In spring 2017, Phil Klygo finally followed through on his original idea of reissuing parts of Art's back catalogue, by putting together a radical revision of the 1991 PolyGram self-titled album, which had long been out of print. Repackaged with new artwork and given the title *Remember Her Name* after its standout opening track, the album now had a new lease on life it rightfully deserved in the digital age.

> This re-release holds a great depth of meaning for me, as it comes twenty-five years after I met and married Sherri at the same time as writing and recording the thing. She is definitely a muse to some of these tracks, "Ruin My Life," "Faithlessly Yours," and to the whole endeavour, really. She is my conscience to this day. We got to go to the south coast of Spain to shoot the videos, and the joy of making them is evident in the performances. My memory holds an unforgettable spot for that time of my life. Have to add to all this love the geopolitics of the time, which have only worsened.

In July 2018, Art returned to Vancouver to once again attempt something new, an acoustic set at the Vancouver Folk Music Festival. Although it took some diehards by surprise, the choice was in line with Art's new-found emphasis on having his lyrics come across as clearly and directly as possible, without being drowned out by amplification.

> Interview with the *North Shore News*, July 13, 2018:
> There's enough people making too much noise now. I just can't bear it anymore, all the racket in the world. My few lyrics that get out there, I don't want them to be overwhelmed by a kick drum or something. I want to make timeless music.

When asked what issues were currently troubling him, Art was quick to mention the European refugee crisis, ongoing environmental degradation—which he was witnessing first-hand in the farmland around Airdrie—and the seeming inability to bring corrupt public officials and corporate leaders to justice. It would all form the basis of his next collection of songs, recorded at the beginning of 2020.

Performing at Blue Frog Studios in White Rock BC, 2016, with Paul Rigby on mandolin. (Dee Lippingwell)

After he and Lorrie Matheson laid down bass and drums tracks at Arch Audio, the onset of Covid-19 meant that any close contact in the studio would be out of the question. Art instead continued the sessions remotely with the help of Russell Broom, one of Calgary's best-known producers and session musicians. Together, they gradually shaped the songs based on the template set by *The Apostate*, but with a greater emphasis on electric guitars that brought out some of the old punk fury where it was needed.

Art named the album *Late Stage Empire Dementia*, after another ten-minute Crazy Horse–style observation of the downfall of western civilization. Essentially a continuation of "Pioneers" from *The Apostate*, the song opened with an ironic, dirge-like reference to the surf-rock classic "California Sun" and proceeded to encapsulate—in brutal detail—the sense of confusion and, above all, comeuppance prevalent during the Trump years and further stoked by the pandemic. "In the plague year of empire / The people finally recognized / What it was like to live in reserve / To be fatally colonized."

It set a high bar for the rest of the album, but Art was more than equal to the challenge on songs like "Entropy," on which thoughts of his father's escape from Russia mingled with the shocking images the west saw of Syrian refugees on overcrowded boats in the Mediterranean, specifically the photo of two-year-old Alan Kurdi lying dead on a beach. There were also the shocking images closer to home of the children of Central American migrants held in cages at the Texas border. Art captured the anger and helplessness it all caused in "Los Desaparecidos (Border Art)," a lament worthy of Woody Guthrie: "Keep your finger on the trigger / Sight on the children that shiver / Like flowers that wave / At the bottom of your wall / May it be your grave."

It was all leading to what Art envisioned in "La Mort de l'Ancien Regime" as a second French Revolution in Washington DC, when "Heads will roll down Pennsylvania Avenue." But he saved his white-hot rage for "Christo-Fascists," the album's standout rocker featuring a rare guest appearance by MC5 guitarist Wayne Kramer, arranged through the San Francisco punk label Porterhouse Records, which had briefly courted Art for its roster. The song encapsulated the summer of 2020 almost too well, from the murder of George Floyd and the rise of white nationalism to the tacit acceptance of all of it by evangelicals, and the unwillingness of the liberal establishment to do anything meaningful to stop it. It was a devastating summation that in many ways brought Art's songwriting back to its origins at a moment when most of his peers had set their musical pursuits on the sidelines.

Although Joe Keithley still led D.O.A. as he always had, his focus had shifted to politics after he became a viable Green Party candidate and finally won a seat on Burnaby city council in 2018. This followed the path taken by Andrew Cash joining his former L'Etranger bandmate Charlie Angus as a New Democratic Party member of Parliament in 2011. Meanwhile, the Vancouver punk mantle had been passed to a new generation of bands such as Japandroids, the Pack A.D., and White Lung, all while rising rents forced the closure of most of Vancouver's vital live-music venues, giving rise to its new moniker "No Fun City."

But with *Late Stage Empire Dementia*, Art found himself back in the national spotlight as the album earned some of the best reviews of his entire career, and he was once again named to the Polaris Prize long list in 2021. There was another reason for the attention, though: late in 2020, Art was notified that he had been named a member of the Order of Canada, the annual honour bestowed upon individuals who have demonstrated an outstanding level of talent and service to Canadians. No one in Art's world could have conceived of something like this ever happening, and indeed it was somewhat surreal to hear Governor General Julie Payette acknowledge Art's "indelible contributions to the Canadian punk music scene, and… his thought-provoking discourse on social, gender and racial inequalities."

At first, Art thought it was possibly a joke made at his expense by an old friend now working in the Governor General's office but once he confirmed it was true, Art responded by saying that he hoped it would help raise awareness of the issues that most troubled him.

> Today, the key thing, I think, is the Canadian government should stop taking First Nations to court and give them fresh drinking water, suitable housing, and to honour the treaties. I have been toiling in the underground for years, and awards like this are kind of anathema. [Punk] meant ultimate freedom, ultimate tearing-down of status quos wherever they might be. [Before that] I was just writing songs and not having any direction. It taught me that there are things to fight against in this world, and you can use music to do it.

Against all odds, Art and Sherri had managed to build a home in Rocky View County, where they doted upon their granddaughter and entertained thoughts of future creative endeavours.

Yet, the cruel hand of fate took Sherri in the early hours of Sunday, March 20, 2022. There was little else that could be said other than words Art and Sherri had written together for "Buried Alive": "Practising nurses offer up the cure / All the liars talk that hang around here / It was the longest day of the year / In my never-ending search for culture and bliss / A cup of coffee and a morning kiss / How could I ever think there was more than this.

"She says so sorry, my whole life's a crime / Roll over me and I'll bury you alive."

Like countless preceding generations, the punks believed they

(ALEX WATERHOUSE-HAYWARD)

could make the world a more tolerant, egalitarian place in their lifetime. Indeed, for a brief period, it did seem like rock and roll could be the catalyst for that change, though only up to the point when it could no longer be hidden that musicians were as fallible as the rest of us, if not more so.

Perhaps that is why there are no happy endings in rock and roll, despite what those charged with crafting its narrative might want us to believe. Like all other art forms, its power resides within a creator's pain, fear, frustration, and grief, all things the world will always provide in large supply. Unlike the vast majority of us, Art Bergmann had found the key to unlock that part of himself early in life, without realizing the burden he would need to bear because of it. Yet his body of work symbolizes what Albert Camus once called "a gift offered to the future"— glimpses of truth we are too often denied, or refuse to acknowledge, that are necessary to accept and understand in order to make it possible to love each other, as Art and Sherri did.

Yes, to many Art Bergmann is a legend, although by its strictest definition, a legend cannot exist in the present tense. As long as he remains capable of facing a new day, the present for Art is, and always will be, tense.

DEATH OF A SIREN

She walks these fields
A hungry ghost
Drinking in sunlight
To overdose
Our kiss the syringe
Cuts through scars
Glimpse of heaven?
Cold night stars

The people here can't see
Weather gone weird
What they don't understand
They condemn in fear
She smiles
They demand her name
"I'm the witch,
You turned to flames"

There is no crack
That lets in the light
There is no light
To bridge this dark divide

Grief is the prize
If you're left alive

"Let's do it your way!"
Our loves hard 'cri de coeur'
Even when pariahs
In our film without a score
Anything less
We kicked out the door
"Weren't you born,
Love's what we're here for!"

There is no crack
That lets in the light
There is no light
To bridge this dark divide

So what can I give
To finally relieve
A song worth nothing
That no one believes
A love larger
Than the national bore
I'd kill the world bank
For one second more

There is no crack
That lets in the light
There is no light
To bridge this dark divide

Grief is the prize
If you stay alive
Always surprised
If alive
Grief is the prize
When you wake

She walks these fields
She walks these fields
She walks the sky
Above the fire

I wanna do it your way

Art Bergmann, June 2022

DISCOGRAPHY

1978

▶ **The Shmorgs**
Shmorgs
STRAY / S101 (VINYL)

A1 – "Ain't So Easy" (Bergmann)
A2 – "Exhortation Rag" (Bergmann)
A3 – "All Down the Drain" (Bergmann)
A4 – "Stray Ravers" (Bergmann/Scherk)
B1 – "So Ya Wanna Be a Shmorg" (Bergmann)
B2 – "Last Party" (Bergmann/Scherk)
B3 – "Take It to the Mountain" (Bergmann/Scherk/Cummins)
B4 – "Sunrise Sunset" (Bergmann/Scherk/Cummins)

Art Bergmann – guitar, vocals
Murphy Farrell – drums, vocals
Dennis Ingvaldson – bass, vocals
Ross Barrett – saxophone
Paul Taylor – additional guitar and vocals
James Lougheed – additional bass

Produced and arranged by the Shmorgs

Recorded by Peter Draper at Soundworks, Victoria BC, and by Si Garber at G.A.S. Lab, Vancouver BC

1979

▶ **The K-Tels**
Various Artists – *Vancouver Complication*
PINNED RECORDS / 79330001 (VINYL)

B2 – "I Hate Music" (Bergmann/Nicholl)

Art Bergmann – guitar, vocals
Jim Bescott – bass, vocals
Barry Taylor – drums

Recorded by Robin Spurgin at Psi-Chord Sound, Vancouver BC
REISSUED 2005 ON SUDDEN DEATH RECORDS / SDR-0057 (CD)

▶ **The K-Tels**

45-rpm single
Quintessence Records / no catalogue number (vinyl)

A1 – "Automan" (Bergmann/Bescott)
B1 – "Don't Tell Me" (Bergmann/Bescott)
B2 – "Where Are You" (Bescott)

Art Bergmann – guitar, vocals
Jim Bescott – bass, vocals
Barry Taylor – drums

Recorded by Robin Spurgin at Psi-Chord Sound, Vancouver BC

▶ **The Braineaters**

The Braineaters
Wrong World Records / no catalogue number (45-rpm vinyl)

A1 – "I, Braineater"
A2 – "Funtime"
A3 – "Last Date"
B1 – "Rock Rock"
B2 – "Edge"

Jim Cummins (Jim Cum) – vocals
John Armstrong (Buck Cherry) – bass
Dave Gregg (Dave By Proxy) – guitar
Ian Tiles (I.T.) – drums
Art Bergmann (Art Bormann) – keyboards

Recorded by Chris Cutress at Sabre Sound, Vancouver BC

1980

▶ **The Young Canadians**

Hawaii
Quintessence Records / qep 1201 (vinyl)

A1 – "Hawaii" (Bergmann/Carpenter)
A2 – "Well, Well, Well" (Bergmann)
B1 – "Hullabaloo Girls" (Bergmann/Bescott)
B2 – "No Escape" (Bergmann/Bescott/Taylor)

Art Bergmann – guitar, vocals

Jim Bescott – bass, vocals
Barry Taylor – drums

Produced by Ted Thomas, Bob Rock, and the Young Canadians at Little Mountain Sound, Burnaby BC

▶ **The Young Canadians**
This Is Your Life
QUINTESSENCE RECORDS / QEP 1205 (VINYL)

A1 – "Data Redux" (Bergmann)
A2 – "Just a Loser" (Bescott)
B1 – "This Is Your Life" (Bescott)
B2 – "Don't Bother Me" (Bergmann)

Art Bergmann – guitar, vocals
Jim Bescott – bass, vocals
Barry Taylor – drums
Horace Ogilvie – viola

Produced by Ted Thomas, Bob Rock, and the Young Canadians at Little Mountain Sound, Burnaby BC

1981

▶ **Los Popularos**
Various Artists – *Bud Luxford Presents*
GRANT RECORDS / GRANT 1 (VINYL)

A1 – "Hacienda" (Armstrong/Bardach/Bergmann/Chobotar/Scherk)

Bill Scherk (Bill Shirt) – vocals
Art Bergmann – acoustic guitar, vocals
John Armstrong (Buck Cherry) – acoustic guitar, vocals
Tony Bardach – acoustic guitar, vocals
Bill Chobotar (Zippy Pinhead) – percussion, vocals

Recorded by Jim Cummins at Gore Avenue, Vancouver BC

▶ **Los Popularos**
45-rpm single
PUERCO-MARIA RECORDS / LP 001 (VINYL)

A – "Working Girls" (Bergmann/Shirt/Cherry/Nicholl)

B – "Mystery to Myself" (Bergmann/Shirt/Nicholl)

Bill Scherk (Bill Shirt) – vocals
Art Bergmann – guitar, piano, vocals
John Armstrong (Buck Cherry) – guitar, vocals
Tony Bardach – bass, vocals
Bill Chobotar (Zippy Pinhead) – drums
Andy Graffiti – synthesizer

Produced by Andy Graffiti at Ocean Sound, Vancouver BC

1982

▶ **Los Popularos**
Born Free
GP Productions / GP 101 (vinyl) and Sensible Record Company / POP 003 (vinyl)

A1 – "Get Out of Your House" (Bergmann/Nicholl/Scherk)
A2 – "Can't Come Back" (Bergmann/Nicholl/Scherk)
B1 – "Don't Say It" (Bergmann/Scherk)
B2 – "Out on the Frontier" (Bergmann/Nicholl/Scherk)

Bill Scherk (Bill Shirt) – vocals
Art Bergmann – guitar, vocals
Tony Bardach – bass, vocals
Bill Chobotar (Zippy Pinhead) – drums
Gord Nicholl – keyboards, guitar

Produced by Los Popularos at Ocean Sound, Vancouver BC

1984

▶ **Poisoned**
Poisoned
Dondub Records / DDUB 1 (cassette)

A1 – "It Won't Last" (Bergmann/Scherk/Nicholl)
A2 – "Emotion (Give Me Some)" (Bergmann)
A3 – "Poisoned" (Bergmann)
A4 – "Virgin Territory" (Bergmann/Scherk/Nicholl)
A5 – "God's Little Gift" (Bergmann/Scherk)
B1 – "Yellow Pages" (Bergmann)

B2 – "Fade to Black" (Bergmann)
B3 – "Deathwatch" (Bergmann)
B4 – "Vultura Freeway" (Bergmann)
B5 – "Gray Area" (Bergmann)

Art Bergmann – guitar, vocals
Peter Draper – guitar
Ted Rich – guitar
James Lougheed – guitar
Gord Nicholl – keyboards
Fred Hamilton – synthesizer
Taylor Nelson Little – drums
Barry Taylor – drums
Andy Graffiti – drums
Ron Allan – bass
Kelly Cook – bass
Mike Kernaghan – bass
Bill Scherk – backing vocals
Nick Jones – backing vocals
Randy Carpenter – backing vocals

Produced by Art Bergmann, with Gord Nicholl and Cec English, at Civilian Studios, Vancouver BC

1985

▶ **Poisoned**
Poisoned
EAST-RAY MUSIC / WRC2-3946 (VINYL)

A1 – "It Won't Last" (Bergmann/Scherk/Nicholl)
A2 – "Emotion (Give Me Some)" (Bergmann)
A3 – "Pretty Beat" (Bergmann/Rich)
B1 – "Yea, I Guess" (Bergmann)
B2 – "Yellow Pages" (Bergmann)
B3 – "Guns and Heroin" (Bergmann)

Art Bergmann – guitar, vocals
Tom Upex – keyboards
Murray Andrishak – bass
Taylor Nelson Little – drums
Virginia McKendry – backing vocals

Nick Jones – backing vocals

Produced by Poisoned at Profile Studios and Mushroom Studios, Vancouver BC

1986

▶ **Poisoned**
Poisoned
EAST-RAY MUSIC / NO CATALOGUE NUMBER (CASSETTE)

A1 – "To Tell the Truth" (Bergmann)
A2 – "Blackhearts" (Bergmann)
B1 – "My Empty House" (Bergmann)
B2 – "Runaway Train" (Bergmann/Nicholl)

Art Bergmann – guitar, vocals
Ray Fulber – bass
Gord Nicholl – keyboards
Taylor Nelson Little – drums
Susann Richter – backing vocals, percussion
Paul Hyde – backing vocals

Produced by Poisoned and Paul Hyde at Profile Studios, Vancouver BC

1988

▶ **Art Bergmann**
Crawl with Me
DUKE STREET RECORDS / DSBBD 31046 (VINYL, CASSETTE, CD)

01 – "My Empty House" (Bergmann)
02 – "Our Little Secret" (Bergmann)
03 – "(We Want) The Most Wanted Man in Town" (Bergmann)
04 – "Don't Be Late" (Bergmann)
05 – "Runaway Train" (Bergmann/Nicholl)
06 – "Final Cliche" (Bergmann)
07 – "Crawl with Me" (Bergmann)
08 – "The Junkie Don't Care" (Bergmann/Nicholl)
09 – "Ill Repute" (Bergmann)
10 – "Inside Your Love" (Bergmann)
11 – "Charity" (Bergmann)

Art Bergmann – guitar, vocals
Ray Fulber – bass
Susann Richter – keyboards, backing vocals
Taylor Nelson Little – drums

Produced by John Cale at Manta Sound, Toronto ON

▶ **Art Bergmann**
"Our Little Secret" / "Charity"
DUKE STREET RECORDS / 71046-E (45-RPM SINGLE)

▶ **Art Bergmann**
A Sample of Art
DUKE STREET RECORDS / DSR 8822 (12-INCH 45-RPM PROMO VINYL)

A1 – "Runaway Train" (Bergmann/Nicholl)
A2 – "Our Little Secret" (Bergmann)
B1 – "An Open-Ended Interview with Art Bergmann"

▶ **Art Bergmann**
A Sample of Art
DUKE STREET RECORDS / DSR 8823 (PROMO CASSETTE)

01 – "Runaway Train" (Bergmann/Nicholl)
02 – "Final Cliche" (Bergmann)
03 – "Our Little Secret" (Bergmann)
04 – "(We Want) The Most Wanted Man in Town" (Bergmann)

Track list is the same on sides A and B.

1989

▶ **Art Bergmann**
"Final Cliche" / "Don't Be Late"
DUKE STREET RECORDS / 91046 (45-RPM PROMO SINGLE)

1990

▶ **Art Bergmann**
Various Artists – *Terminal City Ricochet Original Motion Picture Soundtrack*
ALTERNATIVE TENTACLES / VIRUS 75 (VINYL, CD)

06 – "War Party" (Bergmann)

Art Bergmann – guitar, vocals
Ray Fulber – bass
Susann Richter – keyboards, backing vocals
Taylor Nelson Little – drums

Produced by Chris Wardman at Profile Studios, Vancouver BC

▶ **Art Bergmann**
Sexual Roulette
DUKE STREET RECORDS / DSRD-31062 (VINYL, CASSETTE, CD)

01 – "Bound for Vegas" (Bergmann)
02 – "Sexual Roulette" (Bergmann)
03 – "Bar of Pain" (Bergmann/Richter)
04 – "The Hospital Song" (Bergmann)
05 – "Sleep" (Bergmann)
06 – "Dirge No. 1" (Bergmann)
07 – "Swamp Food Thing" (Bergmann)
08 – "Gambol" (Bergmann)
09 – "(She) Hit Me" (Bergmann)
10 – "More Blue Shock" (Bergmann)
11 – "Deathwatch" (Bergmann)

Art Bergmann – guitar, vocals
Ray Fulber – bass
Susann Richter – keyboards, backing vocals
Taylor Nelson Little – drums
Chris Wardman – additional guitar
Jack DeKeyzer – slide guitar on "Swamp Food Thing"

Produced by Chris Wardman at Profile Studios, Vancouver BC

▶ **Art Bergmann**
"The Hospital Song" / "Dirge No. 1"
DUKE STREET RECORDS / DSRD-9040 (CD PROMO SINGLE)

1991

▶ **Art Bergmann**
Art Bergmann
POLYGRAM CANADA / 511067 (CD, CASSETTE)

01 – "Remember Her Name" (Bergmann)
02 – "American Wife" (Bergmann/Koch)
03 – "Message from Paul" (Bergmann)
04 – "Faithlessly Yours" (Bergmann)
05 – "Crackin' Up" (Bergmann)
06 – "If She Could Sing" (Bergmann)
07 – "Baby Needs Oil" (Bergmann)
08 – "I Can't Change This World" (Bergmann)
09 – "Ruin My Life" (Bergmann)
10 – "God's Little Gift" (Bergmann)

Art Bergmann – guitar, vocals
Chris Wardman – guitar, backing vocals
Jason Sniderman – keyboards
Jamey Koch – bass, backing vocals
Joel Anderson – drums
Laura Hubert – backing vocals
Cassandra Vasik – backing vocals
Paul MacAusland – backing vocals

Produced by Chris Wardman at Manta Sound, Toronto ON

▶ **Art Bergmann**
Art Bergmann
POLYGRAM CANADA / PROC 91 (PROMO CASSETTE)

01 – "Faithlessly Yours" (Bergmann)
02 – "God's Little Gift" (Bergmann)
03 – "If She Could Sing" (Bergmann)
04 – "American Wife" (Bergmann/Koch)
05 – "Message from Paul" (Bergmann)

Track list is the same on sides A and B.

▶ **Art Bergmann**
"Faithlessly Yours"
POLYGRAM CANADA / CDP552 (CD PROMO SINGLE)

▶ **Art Bergmann**
"If She Could Sing"
POLYGRAM CANADA / PCD 100 (CD PROMO SINGLE)

▶ **Various Artists**
Last Call: Vancouver Independent Music 1977–1988
ZULU RECORDS / ZULU 5-2 (CD)

1-13 – The Young Canadians / "Hawaii" (Bergmann/Carpenter)
1-25 – Los Popularos / "Can't Come Back" (Bergmann/Scherk/Nicholl)
2-15 – Poisoned / "To Tell the Truth" (Bergmann)

1992

▶ **Art Bergmann**
"Message from Paul" / "Message from Art—Interview"
POLYGRAM CANADA / PCD 108 (CD PROMO SINGLE)

1994

▶ **The Lowest of the Low**
Hallucigenia
A&M RECORDS / 314540228 (CD, CASSETTE)

08 – "Beer, Graffiti Walls…" (Hawkins)

Art Bergmann – backing vocals

▶ **Art Bergmann & One Free Fall**
Various Artists – *Borrowed Tunes (A Tribute to Neil Young)*
SONY MUSIC / Z2K 80199 (CD, CASSETTE)

2-17 – "Prisoners of Rock 'n Roll" (Young)

Art Bergmann – guitar, vocals
Ken MacNeil – vocals
Sandy Graham – guitar
Jim Moore – bass
Bob Vespaziani – drums
Jason Sniderman – keyboards

Produced by Chris Wardman at Sony Music Studios, Toronto ON

▶ **Art Bergmann**
Selections from *What Fresh Hell Is This?*
EPIC RECORDS / CDNK 1028

01 – "Guns and Heroin" (previously unreleased live version) (Bergmann)
02 – "Contract" (Bergmann/Wardman)
03 – "Demolished" (Bergmann)

Art Bergmann – guitar, vocals
Chris Wardman – guitar
Dave Genn – keyboards
Don Binns – bass
Adam Drake – drums

Produced by Chris Wardman at Sony Music Studios, Toronto ON

1995

▶ **Art Bergmann**
What Fresh Hell Is This?
EPIC RECORDS / EK 80208 (CD, CASSETTE)

01 – "Beatles in Hollywood" (Bergmann)
02 – "Another Train Song" (Bergmann)
03 – "In Betweens" (Bergmann)
04 – "Buried Alive" (Bergmann/Decembrini/Wardman)
05 – "Guns and Heroin" (Bergmann)
06 – "Some Fresh Hell" (Bergmann)
07 – "Contract" (Bergmann/Wardman)
08 – "Jones" (Bergmann)
09 – "Demolished" (Bergmann)
10 – "Nearer My God to Thee" (Bergmann)
11 – "Dive" (Bergmann)
12 – "Stop the Time" (Bergmann)

Art Bergmann – guitar, vocals
Chris Wardman – guitar
Dave Genn – keyboards
Don Binns – bass
Adam Drake – drums
Anne Bourne – cello
Ron Hawkins – backing vocals
Stephen Stanley – backing vocals
Jim Moore – bass on "Beatles in Hollywood"

Produced by Chris Wardman at Sony Music Studios, Toronto ON

▶ **Art Bergmann**
"Contract"
EPIC RECORDS / CDNK 1038 (CD PROMO SINGLE)

▶ **Art Bergmann**
"Buried Alive" (radio edit) / "Buried Alive"
EPIC RECORDS / CDNK 1062 (CD PROMO SINGLE)

▶ **The Young Canadians**
No Escape
ZULU RECORDS / ZULU 14-2 (CD)

01 – "I Hate Music" (Bergmann/Nicholl)
02 – "Automan" (Bergmann/Bescott)
03 – "Don't Tell Me" (Bergmann/Bescott)
04 – "Where Are You" (Bescott)
05 – "Hawaii" (Bergmann/Carpenter)
06 – "Well, Well, Well" (Bergmann)
07 – "Hullabaloo Girls" (Bergmann/Bescott)
08 – "No Escape" (Bergmann/Bescott/Taylor)
09 – "Data Redux" (Bergmann)
10 – "Just a Loser" (Bescott)
11 – "This Is Your Life" (Bescott)
12 – "Don't Bother Me" (Bergmann)
13 – "Son of Spam" (live at O'Hara's 1979) (Bergmann)
14 – "Can't Be Denied" (live at O'Hara's 1979) (Bergmann)
15 – "A Question of Temperature" (live at Gary Taylor's Rock Room 1979) (Appel/Schung/Henny)
16 – "Wait for Your Approval" (live at Gary Taylor's Rock Room 1979) (Bergmann)
17 – "Fuck Your Society" (live at Gary Taylor's Rock Room 1979) (Bergmann)
18 – "Beg, Borrow or Steal" (live 1980) (Bergmann)
19 – "Last Tango (Femme Fatale)" (live 1980) (Bergmann)
20 – "Picture of Health" (live at Gary Taylor's Rock Room 1980) (Bergmann)
21 – "Poison of Thought" (live at Lotus Gardens Hotel 1980) (Bergmann)
22 – "The Remainder" (live at Gary Taylor's Rock Room 1980) (Bergmann)

Art Bergmann – guitar, vocals
Jim Bescott – bass, vocals
Barry Taylor – drums

Compilation produced by Grant McDonagh and Gord Badanic
REISSUED 2005 ON SUDDEN DEATH RECORDS / SDR 0062 (CD)

1997

▶ **Chris Houston**
Evil Twang
SUPERMONO RECORDS / SNMCD010 (CD)

05 – "Just Once for Kicks" (Houston)
07 – "Surfin' on Heroin" (Houston)

Art Bergmann – guitar, backing vocals

Recorded 1989 by Cec English at Profile Studios, Vancouver BC

1998

▶ **Art Bergmann**
Design Flaw
OTHER PEOPLES MUSIC / OPM 2121 (CD)

01 – "Our Little Secret" (Bergmann)
02 – "Crawl with Me" (Bergmann)
03 – "Don't Be Late" (Bergmann)
04 – "The Hospital Song" (Bergmann)
05 – "Sin City" (Parsons/Hillman)
06 – "Faithlessly Yours" (Bergmann)
07 – "Buried Alive" (Bergmann/Decembrini/Wardman)
08 – "(She) Hit Me" (Bergmann)
09 – "More Blue Shock" (Bergmann)
10 – "If She Could Sing" (Bergmann)
11 – "Dive" (Bergmann)
12 – "Hung Out to Dry" (Bergmann)

Art Bergmann – acoustic guitar, vocals
Chris Spedding – electric guitar
Peter J. Moore – harmonica on "(She) Hit Me"

Produced by Peter J. Moore at Beaconsfield Studios, Toronto ON

2000

▶ **Art Bergmann**
Vultura Freeway
AUDIO MONSTER / AM0001 (CD)

Reissue of *Poisoned* / SELF-TITLED CASSETTE (1984)
Reissue produced by Chris Houston

2001

▶ **The Young Canadians**
Joyride on the Western Front
WHITE NOISE RECORDS / WNR 006 2M (CD)

01 – Introduction by Dirk Dirksen
02 – "Mental Instability" (Bescott)
03 – "Beg, Borrow or Steal" (Bergmann)
04 – "Just a Loser" (Bescott)
05 – "Picture of Health" (Bergmann)
06 – "No Escape" (Bergmann/Bescott/Taylor)
07 – "Automan" (Bergmann/Bescott)
08 – "Led On" (Bescott)
09 – "Hawaii" (Bergmann/Carpenter)
10 – "This Is Your Life" (Bescott)
11 – "Data Redux" (Bergmann)

Art Bergmann – guitar, vocals
Jim Bescott – bass, vocals
Barry Taylor – drums

Produced by Terry Hammer and Keith Bollinger
Recorded live October 17, 1980, at Mabuhay Gardens, San Francisco CA
Enhanced CD includes videos for "Automan," "Data Redux," and "Hawaii"

2009

▶ **Art Bergmann**
Lost Art Bergmann
BEARWOOD MUSIC / BM 0109 (CD)

01 – "The Junkie Don't Care" (Bergmann/Nicholl)
02 – "To Tell the Truth" (Bergmann)
03 – "Blackhearts" (Bergmann)
04 – "Who Will Ever Know" (Bergmann)
05 – "Final Cliche" (Bergmann)
06 – "My Empty House" (Bergmann)
07 – "Inside Your Love" (Bergmann)
08 – "Runaway Train" (Bergmann/Nicholl)
09 – "Our Little Secret" (Bergmann)
10 – "Ill Repute" (Bergmann)

Art Bergmann – guitar, vocals
Ray Fulber – bass
Taylor Nelson Little – drums
Gord Nicholl – keyboards
Susann Richter – keyboards, backing vocals
Paul Hyde – backing vocals

Reissue produced by Ray Fulber
Mixed by Bob Rock at Little Mountain Sound, Vancouver BC
Tracks 02, 03, 06, 08 previously released as *Poisoned* / self-titled cassette (1986)
All other tracks recorded 1986 by Rolf Hennemann at Mushroom Studios, Vancouver BC

2014

▶ **Art Bergmann**
Songs for the Underclass
WEEWERK RECORDINGS / (WEEWERK)045 (CD)

01 – "Drones of Democracy" (Bergmann)
02 – "Company Store" (Bergmann)
03 – "Ballad of a Crooked Man" (Bergmann)
04 – "Your Cold Appraising Eye" (Bergmann)

Art Bergmann – guitar, vocals
Lorrie Matheson – keyboards, backing vocals
Scott Munro – bass
Chris Dadge – drums
Joe McCaffery – guitar
Ian Grant – bass, drums
Tim Deacon – mandolin
Emily Burrowes – vocals

Produced by Lorrie Matheson at Arch Audio, Calgary AB

2016

▶ **Art Bergmann**
The Apostate
WEEWERK RECORDINGS / (WEEWERK)046 (CD, VINYL)

01 – "Atheist Prayer" (Bergmann)
02 – "Mirage" (Bergmann)
03 – "Cassandra" (Bergmann/Decembrini)
04 – "The Greatest Story Never Told" (Bergmann)
05 – "Live It Up" (Bergmann)
06 – "A Town Called Mean" (Bergmann)
07 – "Pioneers" (Bergmann)
08 – "The Legend of Bobby Bird" (Bergmann)

Art Bergmann – guitar, vocals
Paul Rigby – guitars, pedal steel guitar, e-bow, mandolin
Lorrie Matheson – guitars, keyboards
Jason Sniderman – keyboards
Ian Grant – drums and percussion
Peter Clarke – bass
Foon Yap – violin
Mike Little – accordion
Natasha Sayer – backing vocals
Emily Triggs – backing vocals
Nikki Valentine – backing vocals

Produced by Lorrie Matheson at Arch Audio, Calgary AB

2017

▶ **Art Bergmann**
Remember Her Name
WEEWERK RECORDINGS / (WEEWERK)047 (CD, VINYL)

Reissue of *Art Bergmann* (1991) / POLYGRAM CANADA / 511067
Includes previously unreleased track "Wide On/Hard Body"
(Bergmann)

2021

▶ **Art Bergmann**
Late Stage Empire Dementia
WEEWERK RECORDINGS / (WEEWERK)061 (DIGITAL, VINYL)

01 – "Entropy" (Bergmann)
02 – "Christo-Fascists" (Bergmann)
03 – "Your Second Amendment" (Bergmann)
04 – "La Mort de l'Ancien Regime" (Bergmann)
05 – "Amphetamine Alberta" (Bergmann)
06 – "Los Desaparecidos (Border Art)" (Bergmann)
07 – "Late Stage Empire Dementia" (Bergmann)
08 – "If… Animals (The Anthropocene)" (Bergmann)

Art Bergmann – guitar, vocals
Russell Broom – guitars, keyboards
Peter Clarke – bass
Ian Grant – drums, percussion
Wayne Kramer – guitar on "Christo-Fascists"
Paul Rigby – guitars, pedal steel guitar, e-bow
Danny Vacon – backing vocals
Kate Stanton – backing vocals

Produced by Art Bergmann and Russell Broom
Drum and bass tracks recorded by Lorrie Matheson at Arch Audio, Calgary AB
All overdubs recorded by Russell Broom at the Broom Closet, Vancouver BC

2022

▶ **Art Bergmann**
"Death Of A Siren"
Weewerk Recordings / (weewerk)/076 (Digital Single)
https://weewerk.bandcamp.com/track/death-of-a-siren-by-art-bergmann

Art Bergmann – Vocals
Russell Broom - Guitars, Bass & Programming
Produced by Art Bergmann & Russell Broom

SOURCES

Author Interviews

Andrishak, Murray (16 September 2021)

Bergmann, Art (4 February 2018; 23 March 2018; and 13 April 2018)

Blais, Donnie (2 December 2021)

Decembrini, Sherri (17 November 2021)

Dekker, Tony (9 December 2021)

Farrell, Murphy (22 June 2021)

Feldman, Sam (2 October 2021)

Fulber, Ray (17 September 2021)

Haley, Heather (20 May 2021)

Harrison, Tom (13 May 2021)

Hawkins, Ron (23 November 2021)

Hayter, Rob (22 August 2021)

Houston, Chris (30 November 2021)

Ingvaldson, Oleene (15 June 2021)

Klygo, Phil (11 December 2021)

Koch, Jamey (10 November 2021)

Laing, Corky (7 November 2021)

Mathers, Randy (11 June 2021)

Mitchell, David (19 May 2021)

Moutenot, Roger (16 July 2021)

Paffe, Brad (9 September 2021)

Panchishin, Art (12 June 2021)

Penner, Michael (24 April 2018, email thread re: Bergmann family history)

Pike, Roy (10 November 2021)

Rogers, Jeff (3 November 2021)

Roth, Mike (16 November 2021)

Taylor, Barry (11 July 2021)

Wardman, Chris (24 October 2021)

Wiseman, Les (6 June 2021)

ARTICLES, BOOKS, ETC.

Armstrong, John (Buck Cherry). Liner notes for the Young Canadians album *No Escape*. Zulu Records, 1995.

Armstrong, John. *Guilty of Everything*. Vancouver: New Star Books. 2001.

Barclay, Michael, Ian A.D. Jack, and Jason Schneider. *Have Not Been the Same: The CanRock Renaissance 1985–1995*. Revised edition. Toronto: ECW Press, 2011.

Bengtson, Ben. "Art Bergmann returns to his old stomping grounds." *North Shore News*, July 13, 2018.

Bergmann, Frank. "A Workingman Serves His Own Master." *Maclean's*, December 1, 1973.

Brunet, Robin. *Red Robinson: The Last Deejay*. Pender Harbour: Harbour Publishing, 2016.

Buckner, Dianne. "Small Business Tips from Riley O'Connor, Chair of Ticket Giant Live Nation." *CBC.ca*, June 1, 2012.

Cale, John, and Victor Bockris. *What's Welsh for Zen: The Autobiography of John Cale*. New York: Bloomsbury, 1998.

Canadian Encyclopedia.ca. "Duke Street Records." February 7, 2006.

Catherall, Robert. "Art Bergmann with the Courtneys & CR Avery September 6 @ Commodore Ballroom." *Discorder*, September 8, 2014.

Chapman, Aaron. *Vancouver After Dark: The Wild History of a City's Nightlife*. Vancouver: Arsenal Pulp Press, 2019.

Chobotar, Bill. "Interview on CITR c. 1983." Courtesy the University of British Columbia Library Open Collections—CITR Audiotapes.

CKOM.com. "Canadian Rock Icon Writes 'The Legend of Bobby Bird' for Sask. Residential School Victim." August 21, 2015.

Culpepper, Mike. "The Rolling Stones Riot, Vancouver, 1972." *Shrineofdreams.wordpress.com*, April 19, 2012.

Cummins, Jim. "Interview on CITR c. 1985." Courtesy the University of British Columbia Library Open Collections—CITR Audiotapes.

Dafoe, Chris. "Mo Da Mu: Learning the Art of Co-operation." *Discorder*, August 1983.

Dafoe, Chris. "Why Isn't This Man a Star?" *Discorder*, July 1984.

Dafoe, Chris. "Bergmann Rocks on Explosive Edge." *Toronto Star*, March 29, 1990.

Delray, Dean. "Norman Perry—President of Perryscope Productions, Music Merchandise Legend." *Let There Be Talk #595*, June 14, 2021.

Denton, Don. "Skulls—First Performance—The Future Face of Vancouver punk." *Dondenton.ca*, December 28, 2009.

Doole, Kerry. "Art Bergmann Talks 'Songs for the Underclass.'" *Exclaim!*, September 3, 2014.

Fabrikant, Geraldine. "Market Place: Polygram Stock Climbs the Charts." *New York Times*, July 9, 1992.

Feniak, Jenny. "Art Bergmann's Rage Has Seasoned Beautifully on New Album." *Edmonton Journal*, May 21, 2021.

Griwkowsky, Fish. "State of the Art Bergmann." *Edmonton Sun*, November 13, 1998.

Haley, Heather. *The Town Slut's Daughter*. Bowen Island: Howe Sound Publishing, 2014.

Harrison, Tom. "How the West Was Won: Booking Agencies and Concert Promotions." *Billboard*, January 27, 1979.

Harrison, Tom. "Art Puts Snarl Back in Rock." *Province* (Vancouver), April 16, 1990.

Harrison, Tom, and Grant McDonagh. Liner notes for *Last Call: Vancouver Independent Music 1977–1988*. Zulu Records, 1991.

Hussein, Aliya. "The History Behind White Rock (and the Actual Rock)." *604Now.com*, February 22, 2018.

Jennings, Nicholas. "Rock and a Hard Place." *Maclean's*, February 20, 1995.

Keithley, Joe. *I, Shithead: A Life in Punk*. Vancouver: Arsenal Pulp Press, 2003.

Klassen, Michael. "J.B. Shayne: A Radio Talent Tuned Out." *Mikeklassen.net*, January 7, 1996.

Konstantino, Dave. "Rat Race: The Active Dog and Ross Carpenter Story plus Interview." *Revolution Rock, Show #307*. CJAM 99.1 FM, July 6, 2010.

Lawrence, Grant. "Positively 4th Avenue: The Rise and Fall of Canada's Hippie Mecca." *Vancouver Courier*, October 19, 2016.

LeBlanc, Larry. "Bergmann Gets Another Chance With Hell." *Billboard*, March 11, 1995.

LeBlanc, Larry. "Interview: Sam Feldman." *CelebrityAccess*, April 17, 2020.

MacInnis, Allan. "Ray Fulber and the Lost Art Bergmann Sessions: Art Bergmann Week Redux." *Alienated in Vancouver*, April 16, 2009.

MacInnis, Allan. "That Time the Clash Played Soccer with a Bunch of Vancouver Punks." *Montecristo Magazine*, February 20, 2020.

MacInnis, Craig. "Bergmann's Art." *Toronto Star*, September 2, 1988.

MacInnis, Craig. "Art Bergmann's Funny Juno Joke." *Toronto Star*, March 10, 1989.

Mackie, John. "Demon Rock: The Dark Visions of Art Bergmann." *Vancouver Sun*, July 9, 1988.

Mackie, John. "Bergmann Wildman." *Vancouver Sun*, May 24, 1990.

Mackie, John. "Juno Whoop-Up." *Vancouver Sun*, March 7, 1991.

Mackie, John. "This Day in History: Aug. 7, 1971." *Vancouver Sun*, August 7, 2012.

Mackie, John. "This Week in History 1979: The Clash Rock the Commodore." *Vancouver Sun*, January 25, 2019.

Mann, Helen. "Punk Rocker Art Bergmann on his Order of Canada Appointment: 'I Just Thought It Was a Joke.'" *As It Happens*, CBC Radio, December 31, 2020.

Mayes, Alison. "Madness or Art?" *Calgary Herald*, May 17, 1990.

McArthur, Bruce. "Review: Vancouver Pop Festival." *Squamish Times*, August 27, 1969.

McDonagh, Grant, and Lynn McDonagh. "K-Tels Interview." *Snot Rag*, March 29, 1979 (courtesy Simon Fraser University Library Vancouver Punk Rock Collection).

McDonald, Bruce, dir. *Highway 61*. Shadow Shows, 1991.

McDonald, Bruce, dir. *Hard Core Logo*. Shadow Shows, 1996.

Mitchell, David J. "Biography." davidjmitchell.ca/about.

Mowat, Bruce. "Nowadays, Bergmann Directs His Own Career." *Hamilton Spectator*, February 27, 1997.

Nardwuar the Human Serviette. "Nardwuar's First Interview Ever! (1985)." *Nardwuar.com*, September 26, 2015.

Neufeld, I.G. "Fraser Valley (British Columbia, Canada)." *Global Anabaptist Mennonite Encyclopedia Online*, 1956, gameo.org/index.php?title=Fraser_Valley_(British_Columbia,_Canada).

Newton, Steve. "Art Bergmann." *Georgia Straight*, April 20, 1990.

Nicholl, Shelley. "Musician Becomes Poisoned." *Western Front*, November 9, 1984.

Pacific Northwest Bands. "The Young Society." pnwbands.com/youngsociety.html.

Pedersen, Andy. "Twenty Years in the Underground: Vancouver's Proto-Punk Art Bergmann Finally Gets to Halifax." Halifax *Daily News*, April 4, 1997.

Penner, Michael. *Mennonite Genealogy with Michael Penner*, mennotree/pennerm/index.htm.

Postmedia News. "How Hells Angels and Criminal Gangs Came to Control Much of the Vancouver Docks." May 9, 2015.

Postmedia News. "Fast Eddie Fryer, Eric Clapton's Ailing Half-Brother, Dreams of Duet from Vancouver's Downtown Eastside." May 22, 2015.

Potter, Greg. "Long Time Coming, but Bergmann Signs with Polygram." *Vancouver Sun*, June 8, 1991.

Punter, Jennie. "Bergmann Getting Back to Gigging." *Toronto Star*, October 14, 1993.

Rayner, Ben. "Bergmann Living Down His Reputation." *Toronto Star*, October 15, 1998.

Rayner, Ben. "Art Bergmann Still Angry After All These Years." *Toronto Star*, October 22, 2014.

Reis, Debby. "Defunct: A Very Abridged History of Vancouver Venues (The Smilin' Buddha Cabaret)." *Discorder*, May 6, 2009.

Rempel, John G. "Makhno, Nestor (1888–1934)." *Global Anabaptist Mennonite Encyclopedia Online*, 1957, gameo.org/index.php?title=Makhno,_Nestor_(1888-1934).

Roberts, Mike. "Twice as Brightly, Half as Long." *Province* (Vancouver), November 3, 1996.

Rose-Martland, Jeff. "Review: Songs for the Underclass." *Huffington Post*, August 27, 2014.

Rosen, Steve. "Bob Rock: I Still Try to Make Great Records." *Ultimate Guitar.com*, September 29, 2014.

Roszell, Shannon. "Art Bergmann: The Wavelength Interview." *Wavelengthmusic.ca*, February 2015

Russwurm, Lani. "Local Origins of the Drug War." *Pasttensevancouver.wordpress.com*, August 28, 2009.

Schneider, Jason. "Art Bergmann (Q&A)." *Exclaim!*, May 12, 2009.

Siemens, Alfred Henry. "Mennonite Settlement in the Lower Fraser Valley." University of British Columbia, 1960, open.library.ubc.ca/soa/cIRcle/collections/ubctheses/831/items/1.0106828.

Smedman, Lisa. "'Jolly' John Tanner." *BC Radio History* (originally published in *Vancouver Courier*, 2005), bcradiohistory.com/Biographies/JohnTanner.htm.

Squamish Times. "Are Rock Festivals Really Necessary?" September 3, 1969.

Sutherland, Sam. *Perfect Youth: The Birth of Canadian Punk*. Toronto: ECW Press, 2012.

Tabata, Susanne, dir. "Bill Scherk on Los Popularos (Webisode)." *Bloodied but Unbowed*. Tabata Productions, 2010.

Tabata, Susanne, dir. "Bud Luxford (Webisode)." *Bloodied but Unbowed*. Tabata Productions, 2010.

Usinger, Mike. "Bloodied but Unbowed Traces Vancouver's Punk History." *Georgia Straight*, May 5, 2010.

Usinger, Mike. "What's in Your Fridge: John Auber Armstrong." *Georgia Straight*, January 6, 2017.

Usinger, Mike. "Loving Reissue of the Young Canadians' Hawaii EP Raises the Question of Who Was Vancouver's Greatest Punk Band." *Georgia Straight*, May 13, 2020.

Valdy. "Rock and Roll Song." *Country Man*. A&M/Haida HL 5101, 1972.

Vancouver Sun and *Province*. "Jim Bescott" (obituary). September 7, 2005.

Walter, Chris. *Misfits & Miscreants: An Oral History of Canadian Punk Rock*. Vancouver: GFY Press, 2018.

Waterhouse-Hayward, Alex. "Art Bergmann & Viper Juice at the Wise Hall." *Blog.alexwaterhousehayward.com*, July 2, 2013.

Williston, Robert. "Museum of Canadian Music: Young Canadians—This Is Your Life (EP)." *Citizenfreak.com* (post date unknown).

Wise, Wyndham. "Bruce McDonald—An Interview." *Take One: Film & Television in Canada*, c. 2004.

Wiseman, Les, and Scott Beadle. "Jim Cummins: I, Braineater." *Thepunkmovie.com/articles/jim-cummins-i-braineater*, April 9, 2010.

Wodskou, Chris. "The Unforgettable Fire Burns at Fed: 54-40." *Imprint* (University of Waterloo), September 23, 1988.

INDEX

ABOUT THE AUTHORS

Jason Schneider has written for *Exclaim!*, the *Globe & Mail*, the *Toronto Star*, *Paste*, *No Depression*, and other publications. He is the co-author of *Have Not Been the Same: The CanRock Renaissance 1985-1995* (ECW Press, 2001), and author of *Whispering Pines: the Northern Roots of American Music* (ECW Press, 2009), and *3,000 Miles* (ECW Press, 2005). He lives in Kitchener, Ontario.

Michael Turner is a Vancouver-based writer who was born and raised on the traditional and unceded lands of the Musqueam, Squamish and Tsleil-Waututh peoples. His most recent book, *9x11: and other poems like Bird, Nine, x and Eleven* (Vancouver: New Star Books, 2018), was a finalist for the Fred Cogswell Award for Excellence in Poetry. You can visit him at mtwebst.blogspot.com. Leave a message, he always writes back.